Becoming an Ally
Breaking the Cycle of Oppression in People

Second Edition

Anne Bishop

Zed Books • London & New York
Fernwood Publishing • Halifax

Cartoons on pages 17 and 145 are copyright © Bob Haverluck, Confessions of a Jailbird: The anti-racism comic book. Winnipeg: Family Life Centre of Winnipeg North. Re-printed with permission.
The song on page 35 is copyright © Leon Rosselson, The World Turned Upside Down (The Diggers' Song). England: Fuse Records (1975). Re-printed with permission.
The article on page 108 is copyright © Carmencita Hernandez and Jane Walsh, Moving toward a new emancipation. Toronto: The Globe and Mail (March 19, 1991). Re-printed with permission.
The power flower on page 130 is copyright © Rick Arnold et al., Educating for a Change. Toronto: Between the Lines (1991). Re-printed with permission.

Editing: Brenda Conroy   Cover photos: Eric Ourique (1960–1997)
Production: Beverley Rach   Cover design: Anne Bishop
Printed and bound in Canada by: Hignell Printing Limited

Published in Canada by Fernwood Publishing
Site 2A, Box 5, 32 Oceanvista Lane
Black Point, Nova Scotia, B0J 1B0
and 324 Clare Avenue, Winnipeg, Manitoba, R3L 1S3
info@fernpub.ca • www.fernwoodpublishing.ca

Published in Australia and New Zealand by: Allen & Unwin
Box 8500, St Leonards, NSW 1590, Australia

Published in the rest of the world excluding Australia and New Zealand by: Zed Books Ltd.,
7 Cynthia St., London N1 9JF, UK and Room 400, 175 Fifth Ave., New York, NY 10010, USA.

Distributed in the USA exclusively by Palgrave Macmillan,
a division of St. Martins Press, LLC, 175 Fifth Ave., New York, 10010, USA.

Zed Books pb ISBN 10: 1-84277-225-2 ISBN 13 : 978-1-84277-225-6
hb ISBN 10: 1-84277-224-4 ISBN 13: 978-1-84277-224-9

Fernwood Publishing Company Limited gratefully acknowledges the financial support of the Government of Canada through the Book Publishing Industry Development Program (BPDIP), the Canada Council for the Arts and the Nova Scotia Department of Tourism and Culture for our publishing program.

A catalogue record for this book is available from the British Library.
Library of Congress Cataloging-in Publication Data is available.

National Library of Canada Cataloguing in Publication Data
Bishop, Anne, 1950-
Becoming an ally: breaking the cycle of oppression in people

2nd ed.
Includes bibliographical references.

ISBN 10: 1-55266-072-9 ISBN 13: 978-1-55266-072-0

1. Oppression (Psychology) 2. Social psychology. 3. Social control. I. Title.

HM251.B57 2002   303.3'3   C2001-904022-9

Contents

For Hélène Moussa, who started me on this path.

About the Author

Anne Bishop discovered sexism when she noticed that professors didn't hear what she said in class. If a male student repeated the point, it suddenly became worthy of attention. Later she went public as a lesbian and discovered what it feels like to be spit at, threatened over the telephone, and told by complete strangers that she was going to hell. She also experienced the reassurance that allies can provide. At the same time as she was reflecting on her own oppression, Anne was becoming increasingly involved in anti-poverty and anti-racism work. This forced her to see herself in another way, as a member of an oppressor group. These contrasting experiences planted the seeds for this book.

Anne completed a BA in Philosophy and Religious Studies in her early twenties. After twenty-five years of life education, she completed a Masters degree two days before her fiftieth birthday. The road in between included travel and work across Canada, in the United States, the United Kingdom, France, Iceland, Malta, Ghana, Togo, Nigeria, Guatemala, El Salvador and Nicaragua.

In her mid-twenties, she spent a year at the Centre for Christian Studies in Toronto intending to become a Deaconess in the United Church of Canada. The Centre's radical and collective approach to education at the time changed her. She became a social activist and left the church. However, it was at the Centre that she learned the social analysis and facilitation skills that have formed the basis of her life's work.

Anne has had two "real jobs" —three years as coordinator of development education for Canadian University Services Overseas (CUSO) and eleven years of teaching adult continuing education. This included an analysis and skill-development program for leaders of low-income and marginalized communities, based on a similar course at the Centre for Christian Studies.

She now makes her living by taking freelance contracts in group facilitation, writing, editing, teaching, research and community development. She has also worked at various times as a camp counsellor and director, fishplant worker, grape picker, union organizer, dog walker, farm worker, seamstress, used clothing store manager, cooperative development officer, and restaurant hostess.

She lives on a small organic farm with her partner and an ever-changing menagerie of sheep, chickens, cats, a dog and a draft horse.

Acknowledgements

Any work like this reflects many interactions, conversations, joint tasks, and ideas bounced back and forth so many times that no one can remember where they began. Some of these exchanges happen face to face, others through written work. It is impossible to thank everyone who took part. However, I would like to thank a few of my special teachers:

Susan George, who suggested I start keeping a journal;

Karen Saum, who pointed out how much can be written in fifteen minutes a day;

Julie Vandervoort, who went over the manuscript of the first edition in great detail, several times;

Fyre Jean Graveline, who helped write the story that introduces Chapter Five.

Wanda Thomas Bernard, Marguerite Cassin, Debbie Castle, Jeanne Fay, Isabelle Knockwood Toney-Shay, Toni Laidlaw, and Diane Maxsym, who read the first edition manuscript and gave me many valuable comments;

my family, particularly my parents, Jean and Rodger Bishop, and my sister Ruth Bishop, who gave me the confidence that is the foundation for my life and work;

my co-counsellors and the Re-evaluation Counselling communities in Toronto, Ottawa, Nova Scotia, and all over the world for their love, support, healing, and excellent analysis of different forms of oppression;

all the many friends who have taught me about their oppression or their particular struggle as allies, including Valerie Farmer Carvery, Arturo and Florrie Chacon, Frances Lappé, Barbara Kannapel and Eileen Paul, Jean and Bernie Knockwood, Faith Boswell, Lucien Royer, Victoria Biyele, Luce-Andrée Gautier, Lily Mah-sen, Toni Gorée, Donna Marshall, Pam Reid, Shirley Glass, Gabriel Epstein, Barbara Harris, Darcelle Upshaw, Elizabeth Doull, Jim McDermott, Alan Williams, Rosamaría Ruiz, Ingrid Mendonça, Shireen Samarasuriya, Ela Bhatt, Rhada Bhatt, Renana Jhabvala,

Evangeline Cain-Grant, Olga Flandez, Philippa Pictou, Candy Yip, Joyce Robart, Terry Sabattis, Teresa and Frances Palliser, my community leadership and community development students, the Henson College Anti-Racism Response and Development Committee, and so many others, some already named above;

the friends and colleagues with whom I developed my analysis of Canada and the world, particularly those who participated in the Centre for Christian Studies, the Ten Days for World Development, the Canadian News Synthesis Project, Oxfam-Canada, CUSO, and the People's Food Commission;

the Coalition for a Non-Racist Society ("the white group"), for their pioneering thought and action as allies;

many people who helped me find references. They are: Michael Bradfield, Beverly Johnson, Blye Frank, Gary Kinsman, Wendy Lill, Murray MacAdam, Lily Mah-Sen, Veronica Marsman, Dorothy Moore, Hélène Moussa, Brian O'Neill, Percy Paris, Verna Thomas, and Colin Stuart;

the supportive people at Fernwood Publishing: Errol Sharpe, Bev Rach, Brenda Conroy and Anne Webb;

Bob Haverluck, for his cartoons;

Eric Ourique, for the cover;

my friends who contributed their beautiful faces to the cover—Jean, Bernie and Catherine Knockwood, Donna, Brandy and Anthony Marshall, Jim Schlay, Alan Williams, Betty Peterson, and Muriel Duckworth;

and Jan, researcher, supporter, critic, source of ideas, friend, life-partner.

Big Words

In the beginning, I had hoped this book could be written using only words that are part of everyday conversation. Above all, I wanted to make it accessible to everyone interested in the topic, no matter what their formal education. However, this did not prove possible. Too many of the concepts do not have precise everyday words. I also had to make some political choices when deciding what words to use. At the back of the book there is a glossary containing brief comments on some of the words and concepts used in this book.

A Note on Internet Resources

In this edition of *Becoming an Ally*, I have included some references to information on the Internet. Whenever possible, I have given a standard publication reference first, since information on the Internet has a way of disappearing as easily as it appears. However, there are some good resources on the Internet, and I didn't want to leave them out. All of the Internet references given were active in October 2001.

Preface to the Second Edition

The first edition of *Becoming an Ally* was published in 1994. Some things have changed since then; some have stayed just the same. Neo-liberalism has visibly spread, making progress on free trade, privatization, and the cutting of social programs. As a result, there is a greater gap between rich and poor, all over the world, than there was seven years ago. In response, there is now an anti-globalization movement that is larger, better coordinated, and more international than ever before. For me, this is a great source of hope.

Unfortunately, seven years later, oppression based on gender, race, ability, sexual orientation, and many other differences among people is still alive and well. It still results from the growing inequalities in our class structure and still plays a role in causing them. Competition is still there as well, between and among those who suffer different forms of oppression.

Since *Becoming an Ally* first appeared, I have received many responses—from people I know and complete strangers, from people who are working only on their own liberation and see *Ally* as something they want their oppressors to read, and from people who are on their own journey of becoming allies. I have taken part in many interesting discussions. Three topics stand out: the distinction between being an ally and taking abuse for your good intentions, the emerging field of diversity education, and above all, conflict in social justice groups. The section of the book on the latter topic stimulated more response than any other.

For this new edition, I have made many small changes and some larger ones. I have tried my best to update the resources in the notes. I have also included several exciting works from authors discovered too late to be incorporated into the original edition or written since, some discovered because people who read *Becoming an Ally* pointed me in the right direction. These include Maude Barlow (1998; and Heather-jane Robertson 1994; and Bruce Campbell 1996; and Tony Clarke 1997, 1998a, 1998b, 2001), Ben Carniol 2000, Susan George (1999; and Fabrizio Sabelli 1994;

and articles posted on her website [http://www.tni.org/george/index.htm]), Margaret Green (1987), Kate Kirkham (1988/89), Jerry Mander (1991, 1996), Linda McQuaig (1995, 1998), and Vandana Shiva (1993, 1997, 1999, 2001).

I have expanded the case study on the Enclosure Movement in Chapter Two. Chapter Three, about the structures that hold oppression in place, has been updated to include a brief summary of recent changes in global corporate capitalism and the resistance to it. Chapter Nine, on educating allies, has been expanded to take into account seven years of reading and experimentation.

I began writing *Ally* because I was concerned about how many people, deeply engaged in the liberation of their own group, seemed not to be able to see their role in oppressing others, and how that comes full circle and perpetuates their own oppression. Like Margaret Green (1987), I don't believe anyone would choose to be an oppressor, but we do so unconsciously out of our scars. I was intrigued by how we reproduce oppression in spite of our best intentions. I was also anxious to communicate my own experience of becoming aware of my oppression, then becoming aware of my role as an oppressor of others. I wanted more people to know how complementary the two processes are. Above all I wanted to create a guidebook for would-be allies.

For a few months after the publication of *Ally*, I felt a great sense of accomplishment. I had said all that I wanted to say. I had summed up about fifteen years of learning and given it to the world. I wondered if I would ever feel that pressing a need to say something again.

However, within a few months, I found myself acting as an ally in a situation where everything I knew about the role was not enough. I had an analysis of the individual journey to becoming an ally, but I was caught in a situation of institutional oppression. I learned quickly that institutions are more than the sum of their parts; their patterns go beyond those of the individuals who participate in them. Understanding something about how oppression becomes encoded into our individual psychological makeup was not enough. I began a new piece of the journey, trying to understand how oppression becomes encoded into our institutions.

As a result, this new edition of *Ally* is intended as the first half of a larger work. I hope to follow it with a new work about institutions. The subtitle of the original edition of *Ally* was *Breaking the Cycle of Oppression*. The subtitle of this second edition is *Breaking the Cycle of Oppression in People*. The subtitle of the sequel will be *Breaking the Cycle of Oppression in Institutions*. They will be intended as a pair.

I hope this new edition of *Becoming an Ally*, soon to be accompanied by a sister-work on oppression in institutions, goes out around the world as the first edition did, bringing back new contacts, colleagues, ideas, and learning. As a first time reader or an old friend from the first edition, may this book stimulate your thinking, move you to action, and give you pleasure.

Anne Bishop

Preface to the First Edition

For several years, I co-led a workshop called "Unlearning Racism."[1] Early on in the process, my Black colleague and I drew a line down the middle of the floor and participants moved back and forth between the "privileged" side and the "exploited" side. First men went to one side, women to the other. Then white people went to one side, people of colour to the other, and so on. Each time, participants were asked to remember an experience which reflected that particular part of their identity. The purpose of the exercise was to help people understand that some groups in society are oppressed and others benefit from that oppression; but, as individuals, we all have experienced both at some point.

As a woman and a lesbian, I am oppressed by the structures and attitudes of the dominant culture in Nova Scotia, where I live. I am also white, anglophone, employed, able-bodied, hearing, born a Canadian citizen, "normal" looking, and not over-weight. These attributes place me on the privileged side of the line. Being middle-aged and "middle class" put me sometimes on one side of the power line, sometimes on the other.

I consider myself amazingly blessed. First, I grew up in a family that was able to give me encouragement, support, and enough to eat. Throughout my life, I have had the loving and challenging friendship of many who were not as protected as I was, who grew up with poverty, racism, deprivation, abuse, and war. They saved me from the *näiveté* and privilege-blindness which otherwise might have remained my outlook. I was also saved by being a lesbian and a woman who came of age in the 1960s.

This book is my attempt to answer some of the big questions of my life: Where does oppression come from? Has it always been with us, just "human nature"? What can we do to change it? What does individual healing have to do with struggles for social justice? What does social justice have to do with individual healing? Why do members of the same oppressed group fight each other, sometimes more viciously than they fight their oppressor? Why do some who experience oppression develop a life-long commitment to fighting oppression, while others turn around and oppress others?

This work is a reflection on my experience. It comes out of my social identity in this place and time. It also grows out of my world-view as a feminist.

I am a community development worker and popular educator.[2] For a time I also worked in the field of international development. Over the past twenty years I have been part of, and worked with, many groups struggling to achieve social justice. My observations on these experiences are the main source of material for this book. Along the way, my thoughts have inter-mingled with those of many other people—sometimes through reading, other times through personal conversations. It would be impossible to trace the origin of every idea contained in these pages. When I have taken material directly from others' work and ideas, recently enough to be able to follow the trail back to the source, I have put a reference in the notes. I have also used the notes to give some starting points for those who would like to explore an idea further through reading, experiential education, or group reflection. I have not made any attempt to back up everything I say with anything beyond my own experience.

This book is intended to be part of a conversation. I look forward to readers' responses. I have so much to learn.

Notes

1. Bishop and Carvery (1994). For ordering information, see Chapter Eight, note #1.
2. See the definition of "Popular Education" in the glossary near the end of this book.

Images: Competitive Oppressions

I am watching a video of the Gay Pride March in New York. On the sidewalk a young Black woman screams at the top of her lungs, over and over again: "The wages of sin is death!"[1]

A feminist friend sighs about her gay boss: "We can't get him to listen to the problems facing women in this organization. All he says is we're not as oppressed as he is."

During a march commemorating victims of the holocaust, a group of gay men came in memory of those who died for their sexual orientation. They are forced to leave the march (Emecheta 1989).

I am sitting at lunch with several friends listening to one member of our party, who is Black, talk at length about how white women are reaping incredible benefits from pay and employment equity and are ignoring the Black people they are leaving behind. I will never deny that racism is often part of white feminism, but I wonder how the many verbal attacks I have witnessed against white women by Black women will ever move either group forward.

During the summer of 1990, we hold a series of rallies in support of the Mohawks who are facing the Canadian army at Oka. The Mohawks are trying to protect their ancient sacred place from becoming a golf course. During his speech, a local First Nation leader attacks all Québécois, calling them "those Frenchmen."

We have an international visitor. A group of low-income single mothers is telling her about some of their organizing work. "Poverty?" she says. "What do you know about poverty? This is nothing."

Note

1. This video clip, only a few seconds long, was included in the introduction to a program on issues facing gay and lesbian people. The program was part of the series, *Out in America*, U.S. Public Broadcasting System, September 1990.

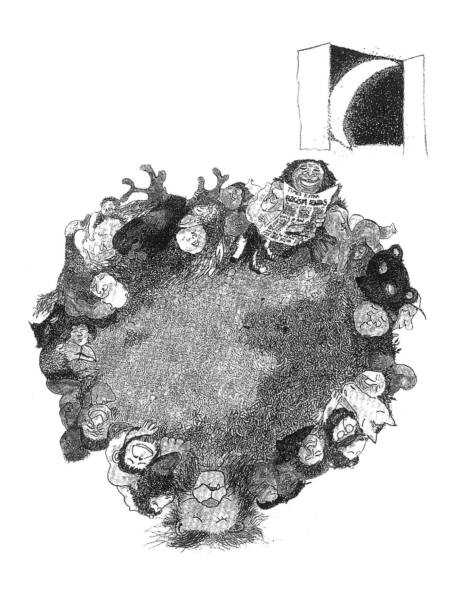

Chapter One

Why Write a Book About Becoming an Ally?

My first reason for writing this book is a dream. This dream is a deep, driving force in me, and I know many others share it. The dream is a vision of the world I would like to live in, a world based on cooperation, negotiation, and universal respect for the innate value of every creature on earth and the Earth herself. This is a world where no one doubts that to hurt anyone or anything is to hurt yourself and those you love most, a world where everyone works to understand how everything we do will affect future generations.

I am what is called an "activist." I like to live my commitment to my dream. I often distrust language, because I am tired of hearing the same words I use—"respect," "cooperation," "justice," "equality," "the people"—with their meaning co-opted by exploiters. However, it is time for me to converse with a wider network than those I can know face to face. I have something I want to say.

I have a vision of how my dream can come about. It is not detailed, because it is not for one person to predict the path of consensus. In general, though, I long to see all of us who are giving our work, ideas, energy, and lives to a society which benefits the rich and powerful rise up together and say: "No more. We can develop social, political, and economic structures that benefit everyone, and we will. We want to take on the challenge of moving towards equality, and we will. We are by far the majority; we can change things."

Between me and my dream stands a high wall. Its name is "Divide and Conquer." We have learned all too well to despise and distrust those who are different from us. Ironically, we have also been taught to despise and distrust people like us. This is because we have been divided even from ourselves. We distrust ourselves. Rather than looking within, to our own thoughts and experience, we accept the word of "the experts."

The second reason for writing this book is anger. Again and again I see examples of division among oppressed people, as in the images at the beginning of this chapter. Incidents like these rob me of hope. How can we take back our world and reorganize it to benefit everyone if we cannot even talk about our different forms of oppression without getting tangled up in the net of competition?

When I see people competing, claiming their own oppression as the "worst," or attacking the gains made by other oppressed groups, I see us all running on a treadmill. As long as we try to end our oppression by rising above others, we are reinforcing each other's oppression, and eventually our own. We are fighting over who has more value, who has less, instead of asking why we must be valued as more or less. We are investing energy in the source of all our oppressions, which is competition itself.[1]

The truth is that each form of oppression is part of a single complex, interrelated, self-perpetuating system. The whole thing rests on a world-view that says we must constantly strive to be better than someone else. Competition assumes that we are separate beings—separate from each other, from other species, from the earth. If we believe we are separate, then we are able to believe we can hurt another being and not suffer ourselves.

Competition also assumes that there is a hierarchy of beings. Those who "win" can take a "higher" position, one with more power and value than those who "lose." It is a short step from accepting hierarchy as natural to assuming that exploitation is just. It becomes right, even admirable, for those who have more power and value to help themselves to the labour, land, resources, culture, possessions, even the bodies, of those who have less power and value. The result is a class system, where power and privilege increase as you go up the ladder, and those standing on each rung take for granted their right to benefit from the labour and resources of those below them. Class will be discussed further in Chapter Five.

As long as we who are fighting oppression continue to play the game of competition with one another, all forms of oppression will continue to exist. No one oppression can be ended without all ending, and this can only happen when we succeed in replacing the assumptions of competition, hierarchy, and separation with cooperation, an understanding that each being has value beyond measure, and the knowledge that we cannot harm anyone or anything without harming ourselves.

The connection between different forms of oppression is often seen in the liberal[2] sense which denies differences, ignores the continuing presence of history, and blames individuals—"We're all the same, all equal, everyone has problems, let's just decide to get along." I have found it difficult, when speaking in public, to say that all oppressions have one root, without my audience hearing me say that all oppressions are the same, or equal. People often feel that their oppression has been belittled. But I am not saying that all oppressions are the same or equal; equality means nothing in this context, for how would you measure? I certainly am not saying that we all have problems and should just learn to get along; this denies a long, complicated history and all the terrible scars that need healing, collectively, before we can live together in peace. What I am saying is that all oppressions are interdependent, they all come from the same world-view, and none can be solved in isolation. We can either perpetuate a society based on competition, where some win and some lose, or we can work toward a society based on cooperation, where winning and losing become irrelevant. In the first scenario, oppression will continue to exist for almost everyone. In the second, it will fade away, because it serves no purpose.

The idea that one form of oppression, or even one person's oppression, can be solved independently is of great benefit to the rich and powerful. This belief is enough to keep oppressed people fighting and jostling in competition with each other, never reaching a point of unity where we can successfully challenge those with more than their share.

Reverend Martin Niemöller, a Nazi prison survivor, recognized this:

> First they arrested the communists—but I was not a Communist, so I did nothing. Then they came for the Social Democrats—but I was not a Social Democrat, so I did nothing. Then they arrested the Trade Unionists—and I did nothing, because I was not one. And then they came for the Jews, and then the Catholics, but I was neither a Jew nor a Catholic, and I did nothing. At last they came and arrested me—and there was no one left to do anything about it. (Bartlett 1980:824)

I regain hope every time I see someone reach out past the boundaries of their own oppression to understand and support someone else's struggle. Hope is my third reason for writing this book.

I have a fourth reason for writing about becoming an ally. Through my own journey of recognizing first my oppression, then my role as an oppressor, I found written work that helped me understand my own oppressions and the process of liberation from each one.[3] I found excellent literature on unlearning racism,[4] and good workshop materials for unlearning heterosexism.[5] I also found a few writers who are working to understand and communicate the complex interrelationship of racism, sexism, heterosexism, and class,[6] and a growing literature of personal accounts by individuals coming to grips with their role as oppressors.[7]

What I have not found is a critical analysis of the relationships among all forms of oppression or of the journey from fighting one's own oppression to forming an alliance with others. Not everyone who is active against his or her own oppression breaks out of the competitiveness and learns to support others. For those who do, what is the process?

In *Yearning: Race, Gender and Cultural Politics,* bell hooks asks for more discussion of the roots of racism in white people and the process of becoming anti-racist:

> One change in direction that would be real cool would be the production of a discourse on race that interrogates whiteness. It would just be so interesting for all those white folks who are giving blacks their take on blackness to let them know what's going on with whiteness. In far too much contemporary writing—though there are some outstanding exceptions—race is always an issue of Otherness that is not white; it is black, brown, yellow, red, purple even. Yet only a persistent, rigorous, and informed critique of whiteness could really determine what forces of denial, fear, and competition are responsible for creating fundamental gaps between professed political commitment to eradicating racism and the participation in the construction of a discourse on race that perpetuates racial domination. Many scholars, critics and writers preface their work by stating that they are white, as though mere acknowledgment of this fact were sufficient, as though it conveyed all we need to know of standpoint, motivation, direction. I think back to my graduate years when many of the feminist professors fiercely resisted the insistence that it was important to examine race and racism. Now many of these very same women are producing scholarship focusing on race and gender. What process enabled their perspectives to shift? Understanding that process is important for the development of solidarity; it can enhance awareness of the epistemological shifts that enable all of us to move in new and oppositional directions. Yet none of these women write articles reflecting on their critical process, showing how their attitudes have changed. (hooks 1990:54)[8]

Knowledge of this process is crucial to overcoming all types of oppression. If we understood how and why some people choose to give up privilege and become allies, we would have an important insight into social change.

The need to understand this process is behind my effort to generalize from my own experience and that of others around me and begin to create a theory of how one becomes an ally to other oppressed people. Becoming an ally is a liberating experience, but very different from liberating your own people and, in some ways, more painful. I want to provide a resource for and open up a conversation with others who are travelling this road with me.

In my experience, there are six steps involved in becoming an ally. They are:

1. understanding oppression, how it came about, how it is held in place, and how it stamps its pattern on the individuals and institutions that continually recreate it;
2. understanding different oppressions, how they are similar, how they differ, how they reinforce one another;
3. consciousness and healing;
4. becoming a worker for your own liberation;
5. becoming an ally;
6. maintaining hope.

The remaining chapters will expand on each of these steps.

Notes

1. For an interesting discussion of competition, see Kohn (1986). Also see the glossary at the back of this book for further comments on the terms "competition" and "separation."
2. See the glossary at the back of the book for a discussion of liberalism and how I use the term.
3. There are many, many books and articles discussing steps to liberation, in general and in relation to specific forms of oppression. I cannot begin to list them here; however, the key to my own understanding of the process was the work of Paulo Freire 1970, 1972, 1973.
4. Some resources for unlearning racism are listed in the bibliography at the end of this book, including Brown (1982), CUSO (1990), James (1989), Jensen (1998, 1999), Katz (1978), Lee (1985), McCaskell (1988), McIntosh (1990), Obedkoff (1989), Thomas and Novogrodsky (1983a, 1983b), and Thomas (1984).
5. A key resource for unlearning heterosexism is the organization, The Campaign to End Homophobia (The Campaign, Box 438316, Chicago, IL,

60643-8316, U.S.A. [http://www.endhomophobia.org] and their publications, Obear (1990) and Thompson (1990). Also see Blumenfeld (1992) and Pharr (1988). Other good resources on the Internet are: Assault on Gay America: The Life and Death of Billy Jack Gaither [http://www.pbs.org/wgbh/pages/frontline/shows/assault] and PFLAG [http://www.pflag.org].

6. Writers I have found who are trying to relate racism, sexism, heterosexism and class are bell hooks, Audre Lorde, Suzanne Pharr, and the "structuralist" school of social work, including Maurice Moreau, Gisèle Legault, Pierre Racine, and Peter Leonard.

7. Excellent examples of white people coming to terms with racism are the Jensen, Katz, McCaskell and McIntosh references in note #4, above. Also see Carniol (2000), Green (1987), Pogrebin (1991) and Helms (1990).

    Good examples of men writing on sexism are Frank (1987), Kaufman (1987), Lyttelton (1983/84), Snodgrass (1977), Tolson (1977). Men's anti-sexist organizations are very active on the World Wide Web. See: European Mixed Group Against Sexism [http://www.geocities.com/CapitolHill/7422], the National Organization of Men Against Sexism [http://www.csbs.ju.edu/mm22/suite.nomas.html], Real Men (Boston) [http://www.cs.utk.edu/~bartley/other/realmen.html], Men's Net [http://infoweb.magi.com/~mensnet], Real Men [http://www.ibd.ncr.ca/~mansfield/feminism/realmen/html], Men for Change [http://www.chebucto.ns.ca/CommunitySuppport/Men4Change/index.htm]. The Men for Change website is also a gateway into the Men Against Violence Webring, a collection of men's anti-sexism websites.

8. Since bell hooks wrote these words in 1990 and I wrote the first edition of *Becoming an Ally* in 1994, there has been a growing interest in understanding whiteness among anti-racist white people. Katz, McCaskell, McIntosh, and Pogrebin (references in note #5, above) were all pioneers in this area. There are also active discussions on the Internet. See Race Relations.About.Com [http://racerelations.about.com/newsissues/racerelations/cs/white privilege/index.htm], Recovering Racists Network [http://], and the Anti-Racism Network [http://www.anti-racism.net].

Web Chart: Conquest of a Peaceful Culture

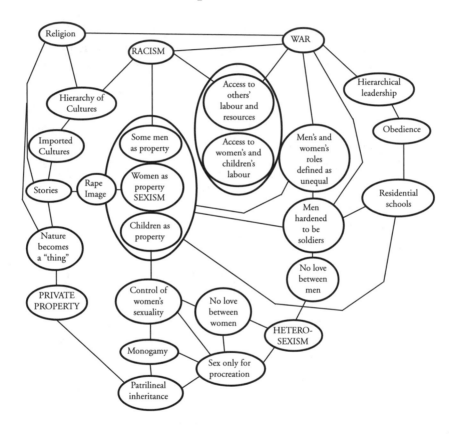

Chapter Two

Step 1: Understanding Oppression— How did it come about?

Sometimes when I am teaching about the dynamics of power and oppression, I have participants do an exercise. We discuss different value systems and how they shape societies. We define separation and connection, hierarchy and equal value, competition and cooperation. They are then divided into small groups and given this task:

> You are a society with a social structure based on separation, hierarchy, and competition. In keeping with your beliefs, you have conquered another nation and taken possession of their land and resources.
>
> The conquered nation has a society based on connection, equal value, and cooperation. Before you came along, they lived in peace, and each person, regardless of gender, age, and ability, had the right to self-determination and everything they needed to live. Since all species and all elements of nature were included in their understanding of connection, equal value, and cooperation, nothing could be owned or exploited the way you do it in your society.
>
> For the time being, you are forcing your system on them, which is not difficult, since they were not prepared to defend themselves; war was incomprehensible in their belief system. However, you do not want to invest in armed occupation forever. You want their next generation to think and behave the way you do and therefore be able to assimilate into your society.
>
> For simplicity's sake, you will assume both societies have the same skin colour.

In order to accomplish the task, I give them flipchart paper and markers. On the first sheet, they list, in two columns, some of the characteristics they would expect to find in the conquered society and the contrasting characteristics of their own imaginary competitive society.

Next, participants decide on a first step to begin the task of assimilation. We use a technique called the "web chart." They write their first tactic near the centre of the paper and circle it. Then they work backward from this first step, that is: "In order to do this, first we must do this." Each idea is written in a new circle and connected to the last one by a short line. They continue for as many steps as they can imagine. Then they go back to all of their circles and work forward, that is: "If we do this, then this will happen." They continue this process as far as they can. Finally, they look at all the steps, forward and backward, and use lines to connect any that are related.

It is fascinating to watch groups work on this task. They start with different tactics. Some, especially if there are First Nations people present, start with residential schools. Groups with feminist women in them sometimes start with taking away women's property rights or introducing the men in the conquered society to the idea of violence against women. Other groups begin with introducing private property or racism or control of sexual and emotional expression.

Wherever the group begins, by the time they have worked their way through all the requirements for and results of their first tactic, many other possible tactics are present on the page. In a very short time, most groups complete a large portion of the whole jigsaw puzzle of oppression. They discover for themselves that no one form of oppression can stand alone without the others and that, as long as the basic assumptions of competition, separation, and hierarchy are present, everything else follows.

Here is an example. Let us follow a group that began by introducing the idea of private property. Their final drawing is reproduced on page 24. Working backwards they came up with the list of steps which follows:

In order to introduce the concept of private property, it will be essential to introduce a belief system that portrays the earth, animals, plants, and resources as "things," separate from large ecological systems, with no value except what they can be used for by their owners. This might require some cultural action, perhaps some stories that glorify the killing, conquest, and domination of nature and the benefits of these activities. What about portraying nature as female and her conquest as rape? A religion that believes humans are superior to nature would be useful, too.

Writers, playwrights, performers, and media people who can write and disseminate these stories may have to come from our culture at first. We must set up systems to import culture.

In order to have rape work as a positive image for oppressors, we must set up its reflection in the society. We must make women into "things," "possessions" to be conquered and dominated, and make sure men get benefits from doing this. The most effective benefit would be to make women the property of men once they are "conquered" by rape and give the man the right to use the woman's labour to make his life easier and wealthier.

Why stop at making women into things to be conquered and used? What about children? The elderly? All those too weak to be conquerors themselves? This idea of defining people as "things" connects back to defining the natural world as "things."

Even men could be property in some cases, but we must be sure that there are clear distinctions between those who can own and those who are designated as property. Easily identifiable differences would be best—like skin colour, height, eye shape, accent when speaking. The owning of other men must give the owners the same benefits as the owning of women—access to their labour. The owners could also take possession of the conquered men's land and resources. This could eventually be developed into full-blown racism.

Even if the property owners don't "own" other human beings outright, and there is no line drawn based on physical appearance or culture, they can control others' labour, because anyone who doesn't have property must work for them. This is the basis of an economic class system—some (usually a minority) own the productive resources, like land, raw materials, and machines. Others (the majority) have no choice but to work for the owners to survive. At this point, the group returned to the circles already on the page and began to work forward from each one:

If we import culture, the result will be a better grasp of a hierarchy of cultures—ours is superior to theirs, others must also be judged and placed in the hierarchy. It would be good to label some as inferior to theirs so they get to take out their frustration at being inferior to us on someone else. This connects back to racism.

Once the idea of getting possession of the labour, land, and resources of "inferior" cultures is firmly established, the next thing we need our conquered people to do is go to war and conquer someone else.

If they go to war, they will have to stop valuing all their people equally and begin to put more value on physical strength, aggression, and mobility, less on nurturing, home-making, and gentleness. This will tend to give greater value to men for their physical strength and devalue women's roles of bearing and breast-feeding children. Men and women will become more role-defined and unequal.

If women become defined by "hearth and home" and men by war, women and those they nurture—children, the weak and the elderly—will become thought of increasingly as in need of men's protection. This helps reinforce the idea that women and other weaker people are men's property and men can rightfully benefit from their labour. In return, men offer weaker folk protection.

When men go to war they must be hardened. Masculinity must be defined as toughness and violence.[1] Men must be able to kill. They also must be able to withstand seeing their companions maimed and killed. They must be able to just step over their comrade's body and go on. This will require the bond between men to change from the friendships they experienced as part of a peaceful culture. They must bond with each other as "brothers" or "comrades" in an abstract sense only. Their loyalty must also be to ideas rather than people—ideas such as country or race. They must not love each other as individuals. This means that love between men must be strongly discouraged. A method of doing this would be to make men who love men one of those male groups that is owned by other men and defined as female, like all other possessed people, and therefore subject to rape and conquest. Now we have part of heterosexism added to the picture.

Another way to make men fight and kill is to establish an absolute hierarchy of leadership and to reward only obedience. This will also give the mobility and speed of response required by war. Hierarchical leadership connects back to a number of other circles. The process of teaching people to value obedience must apply to all the possessed people—women, children, slaves. Also, hierarchy and obedience among individuals reinforces the notion of a hierarchy among peoples inherent in racism.

Some other elements of heterosexism come from the concept of women and children as property. If women and children are the property of men, then each man must be able to control his woman's (or women's) sexuality. This gives him control over her and an assurance that her children are his. The best way to do this would be to stress male-dominated monogamous or polygynous marriage. These types of marriage would be useful in establishing a patrilineal system of inheritance, necessary to allow all of the family property to be passed down from father to son. Men's property rights will be reinforced generally.

Another important step in allowing men to control women's sexuality will be to limit sex to procreation. This is where we connect to the heterosexism circle again. Same-sex love, even friendship, must be suppressed among women as well as men; sexuality-for-procreation-only gives a justification for destroying gay and lesbian people.

Going back to the circle that defines children as possessions, child rearing and education must be done in such a way that this whole network of values is deeply internalized. Children must be taught obedience. They must experience violence so that they will be angry enough to practise violence on others when they can. When they take this step, they must experience the rewards of controlling others through violence. Boys and girls must learn their roles, and children from the dominant culture and other cultures must learn their relative values by reproducing the whole society in the home and school settings. The best way to do this, particularly at first, will be to establish residential schools and remove the children completely from any nurturing elements in their families. Even after the conquering culture is firmly established, residential schools will continue to be a good way to ensure that the ruling elite of men is thoroughly taught the values and practices of competition, separation, and hierarchy.

This example shows how a group starting with private property discovered the necessity of introducing sexism, racism, ageism, adultism, heterosexism, and ableism.[2] I am sure the reader can see how a group starting with something else—residential schools, for example, or the elimination of women's property rights—would also eventually uncover the whole system.[3]

Sometimes I ask the group to reflect on elements that would be added to their assimilation strategies if the conquered people had a different skin colour from the conquerors. Many more aspects of racism emerge from this discussion.

In my experience, this exercise leaves everyone completely depressed. Participants discover how much they know about oppressing others. It is very important to have a full debriefing process when the exercise is finished. People need to be reminded that just knowing the dynamics of oppression well does not mean we are somehow evil. We are children of this network of values. We have learned how it works from our first days, largely unconsciously. It is also important not to leave participants before they have had an opportunity to use what they have learned to build strategies for change.

However, before going on to strategy building, I risk deepening the depression for a short time by having the group reflect on the likelihood of the conquered society resisting these tactics. They usually conclude that at first it would be very difficult, because their social structures, technology, values, and behaviour are all organized around cooperation. They would be most likely to welcome the conquerors as friends and discover the exploitative intentions too late. Later they would likely develop organized resistance, but in order to do that successfully, they would have to reorganize their culture to include the conqueror's competitive values, war technology, and social structures. The resistance might go on for years or even centuries, but the essential nature of the cooperative society would be severely damaged or lost altogether.

The purpose of the exercise I have described is to learn about the complex and necessary interrelationships among different forms of oppression. The scenario is extremely simple and would be unlikely to occur in such a "pure" form. However, there are signs in history, mythology, and archeology that versions of the dynamics described by this educational exercise have happened, in different times and places, all over the world.

No one knows where competitive, conquering societies began, but the earliest archeological evidence of such societies dates from roughly 3500 BCE (Eisler 1990:49; Starhawk 1982:38). This is not very long ago for a species that was living in groups, creating art, and using tools by at least 35000 BCE.

Wherever and however the notion of competition/conquest began, there are numerous stories of contacts between conquering peoples and peaceful, cooperative ones, where the cooperative society was eventually transformed by processes resembling the ones my classes drew on sheets of newsprint. These dynamics also occur within a society when a class or group with competitive social structures becomes strong enough to extend its control to other parts of its own society.

I must leave thorough study of these dynamics to scholars of history, mythology, and archeology, but I want to give three brief examples, based on others' work. The first two illustrate contact between conquering and cooperative peoples, one in Europe from 4300 to 2800 BCE, and the other in North America in the sixteenth century. The third example involves a wealthy class expanding their power over others in their own society. It took place during the sixteenth and seventeenth centuries in England.

I am taking my first example, that of Europe between 4300 and 2800 BCE, from Riane Eisler, *The Chalice and the Blade* (1990:42–54), and Marija Gimbutas, *Goddesses and Gods of Old Europe* (1982:9–10, 17–18) and *The Language of the Goddess* (1989:xix–xxi).

Marija Gimbutas is an archeologist, whose life work was unearthing the remains of the Neolithic period (7000 to 3500 BCE) in what she called

"Old Europe," the area stretching north from the Adriatic and Aegean seas to former Czechoslovakia, southern Poland, and western Ukraine. She organized the thousands of objects found in this area, particularly art objects, to reveal the basic world-view of Old Europe. Using the archeological work of others, she extended her analysis of the artifacts to include western and northern Europe (where the Neolithic period was later, 4500 to 2500 BCE) and the Mediterranean and the Middle East (where the Neolithic period was earlier, 10,000 to 8,000 BCE). In *The Language of the Goddess,* she made the links between her work with artifacts and studies of mythology, folklore, language, and ethnography.

What emerges is a picture of a complex and advanced civilization farming in rich river valleys. The social organization was complicated, with sophisticated religious and governmental organizations and extensive specialization of crafts and roles. They used metal and had written communication.

Above all, she found that the Old Europeans lived in peace and equality. Their cities were located close to good water and soils, with a view over agricultural land. No attention was paid to defensible locations, nor were there walls and fortifications. There is no sign of damage from warfare nor any portrayal of warfare in art. Metal was used for art objects, decoration, and tools, not for weapons. According to the artwork, women played leading roles in every area of life along with men, and a study of grave-goods and housing reveals no difference in wealth to be found between men and women or between classes of people. There are many indications that the society was matrilineal. Eisler has developed the term "gylanic" (by combining gy from gyne, for woman, and an from andros, for man) to describe these gender-equal societies. The greatest deity for the Old European peoples was a Mother-Goddess, the Earth Mother, whose gifts included birth, sustenance, and natural death. Her worship is much older than the Neolithic period. She and her symbols, as catalogued by Gimbutas, can be traced back to Paleolithic art, beginning around 35000 BCE.

However, the peaceful, egalitarian civilizations of Europe were not able to survive. Another people, with a very different world-view, were growing in strength just to the north-east of them, in the area between the Caspian and Black seas. Gimbutas calls these the Kurgan people, after the round burial barrows (kurgan in Russian) that cover the funerary houses of their important males. She identifies them as part of what is called "Proto-Indo-European" culture. The Indo-Europeans are also called the "Aryans."

Kurgan culture was also agricultural but was centred on animal breeding and grazing. The Kurgan people had domesticated the horse, an animal unknown in the Old European cultures, and they were semi-nomadic. They had also developed weapons and war. The horse and weapons featured prominently in their religion, where the central deity was a fierce, angry male warrior who lived in the sky. Images of the warrior-god always show him holding a sword or axe, his belt hung with daggers. They were also male-dominated, hierarchical, authoritarian, and patrilineal.

The Kurgan people began to move across Europe, conquering the peaceful sedentary population there. Gimbutas identified three "waves" of invasion—4300 to 4200 BCE, 3400 to 3200 BCE, and 3000 to 2800 BCE. The archeological records show how the life of Old Europe was transformed. In some Kurgan camps in Europe, the bulk of the female population was not Kurgan, but rather women captured from conquered towns in Old Europe. Men were buried with not only immense wealth arrayed around them, including weapons, but the bodies of their sacrificed wives, children, slaves, and animals as well.

The highly developed culture of Old Europe disappeared. The large towns, paintings, written scripts, temples, sculptures, and thousands of female figurines found in earlier levels are absent in later levels. Settlements became much smaller and were built in defensible positions, with fortifications.

What Gimbutas describes as "hybrid cultures" begin to appear, showing aspects of both the Old European and the Kurgan cultures, although the Kurgan culture dominates. She speculates that this reflects the assimilation of the conquered culture into the conquering one.

A great transformation accompanied the Kurgan invasions into Europe. The indigenous culture, centred on the power to give and nurture life, was gradually changed into a culture dominated by the power to take life. A gender-equal, relatively classless society gradually became a highly stratified, male-dominant one. Although the real, historical process was long and complicated, it seems to reflect some of the same dynamics identified by my students as the origin and interrelationship of different forms of oppression.

My second example took place in North America, during the colonization of North America's First Nations by European invaders. The whole story, again, is long and complicated, and the documentation required to make a complete account would fill rooms and take years to study. I want to give only one quote, albeit a long one. It comes from *The Sacred Hoop: Recovering the Feminine in American Indian Traditions* by Paula Gunn

Allen (1986). She, in turn, quotes extensively from the journal of Father Paul LeJeune, a mid-sixteenth century Jesuit missionary among the Innu (Montagnais-Naskapi) of the St. Lawrence Valley. LeJeune seemed to see clearly the necessity of undermining the power of women, introducing interpersonal violence, changing the treatment of children, and establishing authoritarian male leadership in order to "civilize" (that is, dominate) the "savages." He even foresaw the residential school system that did not appear until three centuries later:

> The Jesuits, under the leadership of Fr. Paul LeJeune ... determined to convert the Montagnais to Christianity, resocialize them, and transform them into peasant-serfs as were the Indians' counterparts in France centuries earlier.
>
> To accomplish this task, the good fathers had to loosen the hold of Montagnais women on tribal policies and to convince both men and women that a woman's proper place was under the authority of her husband and that a man's proper place was under the authority of the priests. The system of vassalage with which the Frenchmen were most familiar required this arrangement.
>
> In pursuit of this end, the priests had to undermine the status of the women, who according to one of LeJeune's reports, had "great power.... A man may promise you something and if he does not keep his promise, he thinks he is sufficiently excused when he tells you that his wife did not wish him to do it." Further, the Jesuit noted the equable relations between husbands and wives among the Montagnais. He commented that "men leave the arrangement of the household to the women, without interfering with them; they cut and decide to give away as they please without making the husband angry. I have never seen my host ask a giddy young woman that he had with him what became of the provisions, although they were disappearing very fast."
>
> Undaunted, Paul LeJeune composed a plan whereby this state of affairs could be put aright. His plan had four parts, which he was certain, would turn the Montagnais into proper, civilized people. He figured that the first requirement was the establishment of permanent settlements and the placement of officially constituted authority in the hands of one person. "Alas!" he mourned. "If someone could stop the wanderings of the Savages, and give authority to one of them to rule the others, we would see them converted and civilized in a short time." More ominously, he

believed that the institution of punishment was essential in Montagnais social relations. How could they understand tyranny and respect it unless they wielded it upon each other and experienced it at each other's hands? He was most distressed that the "Savages," as he termed them, thought physical abuse a terrible crime.

He commented on the "savage" aberration in a number of his reports, emphasizing his position that its cure rested only in the abduction or seduction of the children into attendance at Jesuit-run schools located a good distance from their homes. "The Savages prevent their [children's] instruction; they will not tolerate the chastisement of their children, whatever they may do, they permit only a simple reprimand," he complains.

What he had in mind was more along the lines of torture, imprisonment, battering, neglect, and psychological torment—the educational methods to which Indian children in government and mission schools would be subjected for some time after Conquest was accomplished. Doubtless these methods were required or few would have traded the Montagnais way for the European one. Thus his third goal was subsumed under the "education" of the young.

Last, LeJeune wished to implement a new social system whereby the Montagnais would live within the European family structure with its twin patriarchal institutions of male authority and female fidelity. These would be enforced by the simple expediency of forbidding divorce. He informed the men that in France women do not rule their husbands, information that had been conveyed by various means, including Jesuit education, to other tribes such as the Iroquois and the Cherokee. (Allen 1986:38–40, with quotations from Thwaites 1906:2:77)[4]

This single example of Father LeJeune's observations contains several steps in the transformation of a cooperative, connected, egalitarian social system into a competitive, hierarchical society based on separation. These themes appear over and over again in accounts of the European colonization of North America, particularly those written from a First Nations point of view.[5]

At the same time that Father LeJeune and his colleagues, both religious and secular, were "bringing civilization" to "savages" who lived in a relatively egalitarian way, inseparably connected with an earth that they believed to be alive and female, a similar process was happening in England. The sixteenth and seventeenth centuries were a time of rapid transformation there as the propertied class established its dominance over the rest of the population. Major changes occurred in the economic base, class relations, gender relations, and social and religious values.

My first contact with the story of this period was a song, "The World Turned Upside Down (The Diggers' Song)," by Leon Rosselson:

> In 1649 to St. George's Hill,
> A ragged band they called the Diggers
> came to show the people's will.
> They defied the landlords; they defied the laws.
> They were the dispossessed reclaiming what was theirs.
>
> "We come in peace," they said, "to dig and sow.
> We come to work the lands in common
> and to make the waste ground grow.
> This earth divided we will make whole,
> So it will be a common treasury for all.
>
> The sin of property we do disdain.
> No man has any right to buy and sell the earth for private gain.
> By theft and murder they took the land.
> Now everywhere the walls spring up at their command.
>
> They make the laws to chain us well.
> The clergy dazzle us with heaven
> or they damn us into hell.
> We will not worship the god they serve,
> The god of greed who feeds the rich while the poor folk starve.
>
> We work, we eat together, we need no swords.
> We will not bow to the masters or pay rent unto the lords.
> Still we are free, tho' we are poor.
> You Diggers all stand up for glory, stand up now."
>
> From the men of property, the orders came.
> They sent the hired men and troopers
> to wipe out the Diggers' claim.
> Tear down their cottages, destroy their corn.

They were dispersed, but still the vision lingers on.

You poor take courage, you rich take care.
This earth was made a common treasury
for everyone to share
All things in common, all people one.
"We come in peace," the order came to cut them down.[6]

Curious about the Diggers, I began to search for information. For about twenty years in the mid-seventeenth century, there was "a great overturning, questioning, revaluing, of everything in England" (Hill 1972:12). During what is now called the English Civil War or the English Revolution, Parliament and its army defeated the forces of King Charles I, executed him, and established a republic. Feudal society and its structures of loyalty and dependence came to an end. Eventually a new order was established that suited the gentry and wealthy merchants, "a world safe for businessmen to make profits in" (Hill 1972:12), but not before a period of "glorious flux and intellectual excitement" (12). Various groups of common people came forward trying to establish their own vision of political, religious, and economic equality (11). Some of these were the Levellers, Fifth Monarchists, Baptists, Quakers, Muggletonians, Seekers, Ranters, Anabaptists, Familists, and also the Diggers. Apart from the Baptists and Quakers, these names are little known today because their political and economic solutions to the problems of poor people in their time were swept away when the gentry, king and bishops, along with the newer class of merchants, were re-established in 1660 (11–12, 21–23). As Christopher Hill says:

> There were, we may oversimplify, two revolutions in the mid-seventeenth century England. The one which succeeded estab-lished the sacred rights of property ... gave political power to the propertied ... and removed all impediments to the triumph of the ideology of the men of property—the protestant ethic. There was, however, another revolution which never happened, though from time to time it threatened. This might have established communal property, a far wider democracy in political and legal institutions, might have disestablished the state church and rejected the protes-tant ethic. (1972:12)

In 1648, the disruptions caused by economic change and war were intensified by a disastrous harvest. People were starving. A writer of the time tells us that "the poor did gather in troops of ten, twenty, thirty, in the roads and seized upon corn as it was carrying to market, and divided it among themselves before the owners' faces, telling them they could not starve" (quoted in Hill 1972:86). A contemporary Leveller pamphlet declared that "necessity dissolves all laws and government, and hunger will break through stone walls" (86). Soldiers were being disbanded without payment of wages owed them, causing mutiny in some Parliamentarian regiments, and many felt betrayed when the King was executed in January 1649, and the Republic set up without the social reforms they were fighting for (87).

Against this backdrop, on Sunday, April 1, 1649, a band of about twenty poor labourers began farming common land on St. George's Hill, at the edge of Windsor Great Forest. They called themselves the Diggers, or True Levellers. They identified sin with private property and tried to re-establish the right of poor people to make a living from the land. They invited all to join them, promising them food and clothing, a significant offer in a place accessible to the starving millions of London (87, 89). Their spokesperson, Gerard Winstanley, claimed to have had a vision in a trance telling him to make a public statement that "the earth should be made a common treasury of livelihood to whole mankind" (90). Over the next year, other Digger communities were established in at least nine locations in south and central England, with three more in the planning stages (99, 101). In 1650, when food and money ran short in the original Digger colony, they sent out two emissaries to visit other colonies and groups of sympathizers. Their journey visited thirty-four locations in eight counties (101–2). By the time the first colony was destroyed, there were at least seventy-three men living there with their families (91).

Throughout the year of their existence, the St. George's Hill community was harassed by local landlords. They organized raids and an economic boycott and kept them tied up with a series of expensive legal actions. In April 1650, in a final series of raids, they chased the Diggers out of the area, destroyed their crops, and burned their cottages (90–91).

The Diggers were part of a much longer resistance of the English peasant class to what is now called the "enclosure movement." Enclosure was a long and complex process, starting in the fifteenth century and continuing into the nineteenth, reaching the peak of its impact on peasants from the mid-sixteenth to the mid-eighteenth centuries (Allen 1992:13–15; Mingay, introduction to Gonner 1966:xli; Starhawk 1982:185). At the heart of the enclosure movement were wealthy landlords claiming as their own private property land that had previously been seen as a community resource. "The tradition of looking to the ruling classes for protection [was] broken," and instead, "the eagerness to enclose ... together with the primacy given to legal rights to property, over-rode any scruples that the major interests might have had over the consequences for the poorer elements of the village community" (Mingay 1997: 153–54).

English society was already stratified into classes at the beginning of the sixteenth century and subject to almost continuous warfare, but there were many remnants of the ancient, cooperative societies that had existed in much earlier times. For example, although the land belonged in name to the lords, and tenant farmers paid rent, there was a complex system of "rights of common" that gave peasants access to the food, fuel, medicinal herbs, and building materials available in the fields, marshes, pastures, and forests. Many peasants worked their land communally, making decisions and owning equipment in common, and dividing the harvest. Even the poorest family had at least a cow, a pig, and some poultry, along with access to marsh and forest, to provide food and fuel (Gonner 1966:3, 31, 34; Mingay 1990:14–15; Mingay 1997:34, 126; Starhawk 1982:190–91).

The majority of the population were Christian, but communal festivals still reflected an earlier time. Celebrations of seasonal cycles dated back to Neolithic and some even to Paleolithic times. The beliefs of the common people also came from a much older time. "Common sense" still said that the earth was a sacred living being, the mother of life. Her skin was the soil; her organs included rivers (her bloodstream) and the wind (her breath). Her soul lived in stone and the bones of the ancestors under the ground. Human beings lived on the skin of Mother Earth like micro-organisms live on human skin (Mander 1991:211, summarizing Merchant 1980). Wise women and men, or witches, who practised ancient methods of healing, preventive public health, and midwifery were not only the peasant population's "doctors" but also held important leadership positions in the community. Many kept up the rituals of the ancient traditional religions of Europe. Their knowledge was learned orally and was often extensive. The witches discovered many medicines that are still in use today (Starhawk 1982:202).

However, Western culture was undergoing a profound ideological revolution. The idea was taking hold that the earth is a dead piece of rock, or a machine, valuable only as a raw material for human use. From this basic notion, new understandings emerged. Land was beginning to be thought of as a commodity, to be bought and sold. Mining was permissible if the earth was not a living being (Mander 1991:211–12). Knowledge, too, was being transformed into a commodity to be owned by profession-als trained in a university and licensed to practice. Since women and poor people were excluded from formal education, they were also excluded from the newly emerging professions, such as religious leadership and medicine (Starhawk 1982:200–201).

In the sixteenth century several things also happened to cause the landlords to want the people removed from the land. European markets were flooded with gold and silver from the Americas, causing extreme inflation and making the peasants' low rental payments almost worthless. New markets for agricultural products were emerging in the first industrial areas and in armies fighting in England, continental Europe and America. These products could also be transported over greater distances because of new canals and roads. At the same time, demand was growing for wool in the newly organized English textile industry and in other European coun-tries. There were profits to be made from raising sheep. Mining had also become a profitable pursuit, with markets opening up for coal, iron, lead, copper, stone, and slate. The landowners began to pressure for enclosure and fencing, so that they could use the land for mining or raising sheep, cattle, and crops for sale. They worked to transform the land from a resource with multiple uses for the whole community to private property for private profit (Mingay introduction to Gonner 1966:xli, xlvi; Mingay 1997:32, 34, 44, 48, 149; Starhawk 1982:192–93).

A central piece of this transition was the "extinction of common." There were several legal mechanisms for accomplishing this, and they changed over the long period of time during which enclosure took place (Mingay, introduction to Gonner 1966:xlii; Gonner 1966:43, 71). The end result, however, was the destruction of a system of rights that allowed peasants to take the necessities of life from, or even live on, land that they did not legally own. In the new system, landlords could punish those who tried to take fish and game as poachers, those who tried to collect herbs and berries as trespassers, and those who lived on the land as squatters (Starhawk 1982:193–94; Yelling 1977:227–28).

The destruction of the forests, marshes and wild areas changed the landscape forever and dispossessed whole communities of peasants and craftspeople that had been living self-sufficiently in these areas, far from the laws of the lords and bishops (Hill 1972:35-38). Some were "outlaws" who,

> opposed to the king and his laws … specialized in robbing those
> who ground the faces of the poor, enclosers of commons, usurers

foreclosing on land, builders of iron mills that grub up forests … cheating shop-keepers and vintners, but not rent-racked farmers, needy market folks, labourers, carriers or women. (Hill 1972:35–36)

These "outlaws" have been immortalized for centuries by the Robin Hood ballads.

Other denizens of the forests were those who still followed the ancient pre-Christian traditions of England. Large networks of pagans met there to celebrate their annual cycle of festivals and to study magic and healing. The pagan understanding of the earth and all its life forms as sacred was being violated by new ideas of nature as dead raw material, valuable only when exploited for profit (Hill 1972:38; Starhawk 1982:194, 197).

Oliver Goldsmith, a poet living in the late eighteenth century, wrote of the enclosure movement:

> But times are alter'd; trade's unfeeling train
> Usurp the land and dispossess the swain;
> Along the lawn, where scatter'd hamlets rose,
> Unwieldy wealth, and cumbrous pomp repose.
> Ill fares the land, to hastening ills a prey,
> When wealth accumulates, and men decay:
> Princes and lords may flourish or may fade;
> A breath can make them, as a breath has made;
> But a bold peasantry, the country's pride,
> When once destroy'd, can never be supplied.
> (quoted in Mingay 1997:124)

Then, as now, the dispossession of the poor was justified by labelling the victims as lazy and immoral. As G.E. Mingay says:

> The hastening of profitable reform was fuelled also by contemporary morality. Property-owners were likely to agree with those who saw the commons as a cause of idleness and fecklessness, a means of enabling the poor to live without the discipline of regular full-time work. Some went beyond this and thought that the commons encouraged not merely idleness but also dissipation and crime. (1997:154)

Mingay quotes Matthew Boulton, partner of James Watt in their steam engine works, referring to those living on common land as "idle beggarly wretches, addicted to laziness and crime" (Mingay 1997:44). Mingay also quotes a "well-known agricultural expert," writing in 1798. "In sauntering after his cattle," he says, "the cottager acquired a habit of indolence.... Day labour becomes disgusting to him ... and at length the sale of a half-fed calf, or hog, furnishes the means of adding intemperance to idleness" (Billingsley quoted in Mingay 1997:135). Hill records an Elizabethan surveyor's opinion: "So long as [the cottagers] may be permitted to live in such idleness upon their stock of cattle, they will bend themselves to no kind of labour. Common pasture ... is a ... maintaining of idlers and beggary" (1972:40–41). In a quote reminiscent of modern "poor-bashing" aimed at women on social assistance, an early nineteenth-century commentator on enclosure said that peasant women were "very lazy; they do nothing but bring children and eat cake" (Mingay 1997:155).[7]

Women and children were particularly affected by enclosure. In the old system, women and children were employed in their own homes. While the man of the house worked as a labourer on larger farms, the women and children took care of the cows, pigs, sheep, vegetables, and poultry the family kept on common land and produced the family's food and clothing from them. Once the family was separated from the common land and therefore their livestock, the role of women and children disappeared. Some found work in industry, but a woman could only expect to earn half a man's wages, and children even less (Mingay 1997:135; Starhawk 1982:195).

In many areas the dispossessed peasantry resisted enclosure. There were protests, marches, and public meetings. Resisters pulled down fences and pulled up surveyors' stakes. There were riots in Somerset, Cornwall, Wiltshire, Gloucester, North Devon, and many other areas of the country. Marsh dwellers destroyed drainage systems (Mingay 1997:51–52; Starhawk 1982:196). The Diggers were part of this resistance. Women lost disproportionately more of their livelihood than men did and were also very active in the leadership of resistance actions. In one example the workmen enclosing the moors were "held up by mobs of hostile poor who might number as many as a hundred and fifty, and included women armed with dripping pans" (Mingay 1997:132).

Women who were dispossessed by these economic changes and those who took part in resistance were particularly at risk. Witch hunting reached England in the sixteenth century. Although not as vicious or widespread as the witch hunts on the European continent, the English witch hunt had the effect of spreading fear in peasant communities. It helped destroy the unity that made resistance to enclosure possible by making people afraid of each other, for anyone could accuse someone of being a witch. It also resulted in people channelling the despair and anger accompanying their growing poverty towards women. For this reason, although almost half of the witches were men, the witch hunts were directed almost entirely at women (Starhawk 1982:196–97).

The sixteenth and seventeenth centuries have given us a legacy of property, gender, and class relations that persist into modern times.[8] The story, again, although far more complex than the brief summary I have provided here, shows some of the same processes in operation that appear whenever people with competitive, hierarchical, separation-based values come into contact with people who practise a more connected, cooperative way of life. The end result is that the more cooperative group eventually is forced to absorb and live by the competitive values. The essence of this transition is a transformation in the forms of power used in a society.

Like most other people of my gender and class, I have been afraid of power most of my life. I thought power was automatically evil and that cooperation depended on the refusal to use power. More often, I denied the power I had in many situations. This, I finally realized, is because, like most people formed by a competitive society, I thought power could only mean power over others.

I encountered a much deeper understanding of power in the work of Starhawk (1987:8–20). She defines three kinds of power. "Power-over" is domination or force, the power I had been afraid of. "Power-over" also includes its flip side—rebellion. Rebellion is the reaction of people trying to protect themselves or get some control of a situation where they are being hurt by a person or system with power over them. Rebellion can be a dramatic fighting back or can take the form of quiet manipulation. It is the "power of the powerless," used, for example, by children to control adults even though adults are stronger and, in this culture, are the "owners" of the children. If rebellion succeeds, the roles simply reverse and the situation of "power-over" continues.

There are, however, forms of power which have nothing to do with the domination of others. The first is "power-within." This refers to one's own centredness, one's grounding in one's own beliefs, wisdom, knowledge, skills, culture, and community. The second is "power-with," or power exercised cooperatively among equals. The third is "authority," that is, the wisdom, creativity, or expression of a group's energy by an individual that is recognized and agreed to by others as right at a certain time.

The history of conquest by patriarchal cultures is a lesson in the relationship between "power-over" and "power-with." Cooperative cultures practise "power-with," along with "power-within" and "authority." Decisions are made by consensus, among equals. If one person's views have more weight, it is because of wisdom, experience, or an insight that sums up the group spirit at that time. These unequal forms of power vary in strength, shift from person to person, and can be earned and lost, although they do tend to accumulate with age.

When a culture practising "power-with" meets a culture that practises "power-over," the former group does not stand much of a chance. People from a cooperative culture tend to trust others, make themselves vulnerable, and give with the knowledge that something of value will come back in due time. They assume a connection with others that makes injuring or killing another person very rare. They do not accumulate goods. They do not think in terms of self-defence or distrust. The two cultures are not evenly matched.

On a smaller scale, in an organization, even one person who wants control and uses the methods of "power-over" can destroy an experiment in consensus methods. In my experience, when the controlling manipulations begin, the other members of the group have to choose among three options. The first choice is to band together in complete unity to resist the person's attempt to take over. In the second case, one or more members lead the resistance, entering into a power-struggle, which in turn demands the use of "power-over" tactics and ends the cooperative nature of the group. The third option is to break up for the time being.

The first choice is a good one, but the total agreement required is very difficult to achieve, especially if there is discontent in the group or the person initiating the take-over has done some groundwork and convinced others to support the effort or, as is often the case, people are simply not able to figure out what is happening. Often the person seeking control is not even conscious of what is happening, making it even more difficult for others to see the dynamics. Even if the group is successful in forming a united opposition to the one member who is using power-over methods, consensus decision-making must be abandoned, at least for a time, in favour of majority rule. Otherwise the single member can block consensus forever. Unless this change to majority rule is very conscious and limited, the group may not go back to consensus after the problem is solved.

The second choice is very similar to the usual result of a cooperative culture facing conquest. The resistance may be successful, but the egalitarian, consensus-based nature of the group is sacrificed. The third option is by far the most common.

Too many organizations, successful in establishing internal cooperation for a time, have faced this painful choice. The interaction of "power-over" and "power-with" in groups is discussed further in Chapter Four.

Oppression is an inevitable result of "power-over." In order to end it, our challenge is to discover how we can restore the skills, methods, and culture of "power-with."

Notes

1. See my definition of the term "violence" in the glossary near the back of this book.
2. These terms are defined in the glossary.
3. An account similar to this one, which unravels the net of social values woven around war-making, can be found in Starhawk (1987), Chapter Two "The Dismembering of the World," (47–67). Starhawk also explored these connections in a fictional work, *The Fifth Sacred Thing* (1993).

   There is other interesting material on some of the other connections made in this account: on the relationship between women and the environment, see Merchant (1980); on the relationship between heterosexism and sexism, see Grahn (1984), Pharr (1988), and *New Internationalist* (1989); on the relationships among heterosexism, sexism, conquest, and war, see Altman (1989), Barry (1979, 1985), Brock-Utne (1981), Easlea (1987), Enloe (1983). In *Sexual Suicide* (1973), Brock-Utne quotes George Gilder, writing of training in a Marine boot camp:

   > From the moment one arrives, the drill instructors begin a torrent of misogynistic and anti-individualist abuse. The good things are manly and collective; the despicable are feminine and individual. Virtually every sentence, every description, every lesson embodies this sexual duality, and the female anatomy provides a rich metaphor for every degradation. (from unpaginated transcript)

   Brock-Utne adds the comment: "When you want to create a soldierly group of male killers, that is what you do, you kill the woman in them." Another reflection of the relationship between heterosexism and war is the inscription on the tombstone of Leonard Matlovitch, a gay man who died of AIDS in 1988. The stone stands in the military cemetery in Arlington, Virginia: "They gave me a medal for killing five men, and a dishonourable discharge for loving one."

   On the 16th of February 1992, the Halifax *Daily News* reported that scientists working on non-lethal weapons were running into resistance from those at the Pentagon who think that non-lethal weapons are not manly enough, because masculine means killing: see: "A Kinder, Gentler Kind of Warfare; The Pentagon is Currently Studying the Potential of Non-lethal

Weapons." A similar connection appeared in the Halifax paper, *The Mail Star*, 28 September 1992. "The Tailhook Affair: U.S. Navy Lands Its Biggest Scandal" describes the rape and harassment of female officers and some civilian female passers-by at a party held to thank troops for their work in the Gulf War. Some of the high-ranking Navy personnel quoted feel that to curb such behaviour would demoralize the male officers.

Some references on men conquering other men by rape can be found in Barnett (1979), Cole (1989), Hanmer and Maynard (1987), Kleinberg (1987:131), MacKinnon (1987), Troiden (1988), and Mies and Shiva (1993:122–23, 129–130).

4. There is a similar but more recent and scientific account contrasting the high status of women and the gentle rearing of children in a "primitive" society with the subservience of women and punishment of children in Western "civilization" in Bronislaw Malinowski's classic anthropological study of Triobrand society (Papua New Guinea), *Sex and Repression in Savage Society* (1927:25–39).

5. Ronald Wright has collected and studied post-colonial accounts by First Nations people. In *Stolen Continents: The "New World" Through Indian Eyes* (1992), he has told the story of the European conquest of five First Nations from their point of view. The Nations represented are: Aztec, Maya, Inca, Cherokee, and Iroquois.

6. Leon Rosselson (Wembley Park, Middlesex, U.K.: Fuse Records, 1975). The song can be heard on Rosselson's recordings "For the Good of the Nation" and "That's Not the Way It's Got to Be." It is also on Dick Gaughan's "A Handful of Earth," Billy Bragg's "Between the Wars," and "Aya! A Benefit Tape for AIDS Vancouver" by the Vancouver trio Aya (Slim Evans Records and Tapes, 2149 Parker St., Vancouver, BC, V5L 2L6).

7. For an analysis of modern "poor-bashing" in Canada see Swanson (2001a).

8. The process of breaking people's connections with the earth and the re-sources they need for life continues, of course, to this day. For a powerful account of a modern "enclosure movement" and the meaning of the bonds that are broken, see Vandana Shiva, "Homelessness in the Global Village," in Mies and Shiva (1993:98–107).

A Journal Entry:
"They Wouldn't be Able to Pick Us Off One by One"

January 21, 1992

Pearline Oliver, a leader in Nova Scotia's Black community, was interviewed on CBC this afternoon. She is a founder of the Black United Front of Nova Scotia, but said she would like to see BUF change its name and become a people's movement against poverty and social problems. The interviewer argued, more than once, that every "special interest group" has its own advocacy organization; Black people would risk having no one to speak for them. Oliver responded that if people were united, "they wouldn't be able to pick us off one by one."

Chapter Three

Step 1: Understanding Oppression—
How is it held in place?

This book is about the relationships between people experiencing different forms of oppression. My aim is to uncover what we need to achieve understanding based on our mutual dispossession. I believe we need unity to create a power base strong enough to change the system we live in. I spend very little time in this book speaking of those who are benefitting from and actively promoting our oppressions and the divisions between us. It may at times sound as if I am forgetting about them and suggesting that we, the exploited, are to blame for our situation because we keep ourselves and each other down. We certainly help keep ourselves and each other down. We reproduce the social, economic, and political system that formed us by playing out our internalized oppression against ourselves and each other. However, I do not mean to suggest that our mutual oppression is the whole story.

The backdrop for any discussion of oppression is an understanding of class. In all three of the case studies in Chapter Two, a small but powerful group expropriated for themselves resources that were formerly used to maintain life, community, and culture for all or most of the population. This is how class functions. Class is both the result and the foundation of all other forms of oppression.

In the twenty-first century, the elite classes are still grabbing at even more control of the world's natural resources, along with human life and labour, to benefit only themselves. Our "rights of common" are still being "extinguished" as what is left in the public realm is turned into private property. Our transportation infrastructure—including even the sea bed under our harbours—our formerly public parks, public meeting places, prisons, public services, the seeds we grow, even our human genetic code are all being declared private property and sold to the highest bidder. In Canada, our public health care system, something we have fought for and treasured for forty years, is under intense attack. Our federal and provincial governments are carrying out the destruction, but the benefits of the process go to the private health and insurance companies.

In our time, the driving force of this process, the structure of the elite classes, takes the form of transnational corporations and financial institutions. They have woven a web of control around the world. They are using their overwhelming influence with powerful international organizations like the International Monetary Fund, the World Bank, the World Trade Organization, the European Union, and the G8 to move themselves beyond the regulating powers of any national government, let alone the people caught in their web.[1] Renato Ruggerio, former head of the World Trade Organization has said: "There is a surplus of democracy in the world which is interfering with the free movement of capital and investment."[2]

In *Global Reach*, Richard Barnet and Ronald Muller describe the top managers of multinational corporations as "world managers" because they are "the first men in history to make a credible attempt at managing the world as an integrated unit" (Barnet and Muller 1974, quoted in Morgan 1979:275). On the other hand, these "world managers" cannot have a grip on everything. As Malvina Reynolds wrote in one of her songs: "They've got the world in their pocket, but the pocket's got a hole" (1975).

Am I evoking a "conspiracy theory"? Unfortunately, the multinationals do not need a conspiracy to coordinate their activities. In the introduction to A *Fate Worse Than Debt*, Susan George explains:

> I DON'T BELIEVE IN THE CONSPIRACY THEORY OF HISTORY. I take special pains to state this, because I've been accused of just such beliefs the moment I pointed out that a great many forces were converging in a single direction. They don't have to conspire if they have the same world-view, aspire to similar goals, and take concerted steps to attain them. (1988:5)

For decades it seemed as if only a small network of people could see this process happening around us and understand its potential to inflict damage on human societies and nature. However, that is changing. While I have been working on this second edition of *Becoming an Ally*, the United Nation's Intergovernmental Panel on Climate Change has released a report from seven hundred of the world's leading climate scientists, representing a hundred countries, predicting that global warming will have extensive and severe impact in this century. For years scientists have debated back and forth about the existence of global warming. Now few seem to be arguing.

In another report issued a month or so earlier, they also agreed that the cause of global warming is human activity, especially the burning of fossil fuels, and that the impact will fall disproportionately on the poor (International Panel on Climate Change 2001).

As I worked on this chapter, the Summit of the Americas took place in Québec City. I received verbal accounts and e-mails from friends and relatives who took part in the demonstrations against the proposed Free Trade Area of the Americas. Hundreds of protesters travelled to Québec. There was a tiny handful advocating violence, but they were overwhelmed by the huge majority that came to take part in peaceful demonstrations. The police, however, indiscriminately tear gassed the crowd and shot fleeing protesters with rubber bullets. They even gassed the protest media centre set up to serve the alternative media covering the event. Four hundred protesters were imprisoned.

On the Saturday of the Québec City meetings, hundreds more protesters marched in the streets of Canadian towns and cities all across the country to support those who were able to attend the main event in Québec. About fifty of us walked down the main street of Wolfville, Nova Scotia, a major demonstration for a small Maritime town.

Long before the protesters arrived, Québec City was made into a fortress well beyond its famous eighteenth century walls. Security forces surrounded the old town with a two-metre-high concrete and razor-wire fence. Police were brought in from the RCMP, the Surété du Québec, and two municipal police forces. The police booked all hotel rooms within a 150-mile radius and a 600-cell prison was emptied to receive those they planned to arrest.[3]

Meanwhile, the transnational corporations had little difficulty getting the ear of the thirty-four heads of state who attended the meetings. They could advertise at coffee breaks and evening receptions, give welcoming speeches, and mingle with the delegates at networking events. They were given this access in return for sponsoring breaks and events with price tags ranging from $150,000 to $1.5 million (Canadian Press Newswires, April 20 and 21, 2001).

As a result of the protests, delegates at the meeting made a series of public statements about alleviating poverty in the Americas and benefitting all people. However, the core of the agreement is the clause that gives transnational corporations the right to sue governments for interfering with their ability to make a profit. The day after the meeting, the Prime Minister of Canada announced that this clause was central to free trade in the Americas and could not be tampered with.[4]

Just days before the Summit of the Americas opened, the newspapers carried a tiny story in a back corner reporting that United Parcel Service, a large transnational courier company, is taking the Canadian government to task under the North American Free Trade Agreement. They claim Canada is interfering with the company's profits by allowing Canada Post to operate a parcel courier service. If they win, the taxpayers of Canada will owe United Parcel Service $100 million in compensation.[5]

This is only one of a series of cases that have gone to the trade tribunal set up under the North American Free Trade Agreement, the model for the Free Trade Area of the Americas. The Ethyl Corporation sued Canada for banning the use of MMT, a gasoline additive, because it is hazardous to human health and the environment. Canada lifted the ban on MMT and paid Ethyl Corporation U.S. $13 million in damages. Sun Belt Water Inc. of California is claiming U.S. $10.5 billion in compensation because the British Columbia government has banned bulk water exports. S.D. Meyers Inc. wants Canada to pay U.S. $20 million in damages for banning PCBs.

Québec City is one of a series of protests against the transnational corporations and their agenda for the world. Hundreds of people protested at the World Trade Organization meeting in Seattle, Washington, November/December 1999. Large protests also greeted the International Monetary Fund/World Bank meetings in Washington, DC, in April 2000, and Prague, Czechoslovakia, in September 2000. The Europan Union drew protesters to its June 2001 meeting in Gothenburg, Sweden, and the European Economic Summit at Salzburg, Austria, in July 2001. Protesters gathered at the Global Forum Conference of Government and Technology Leaders meeting in Naples, Italy, in March 2001 and the G8 Summit in Genoa, Italy, also in July 2001. Canada alone saw three protests in 2000, at the World Petroleum Congress in Calgary, Alberta, in May, the Organization of American States in Windsor, Ontario, in June, and the North Atlantic Treaty Organization in Victoria, British Columbia, in October.[7] The Organization for Economic Cooperation and Development abandoned its Multinational Agreement on Investment, called "the constitution of a single global economy" by the Director General of the World Trade Organization, in October 1998, because of strong resistance in several key countries, including Canada and France.[8]

Whenever reporters have given the leaders of these protests a few seconds of air-time or print-space, I have been impressed by their clarity. They always make the point that they are not opposed to trade but to the growing control of the transnational corporations over all aspects of life and to the destruction of the environment. Ever since the draft Multilateral Agreement on Investment was leaked to the public via the Internet in April 1998, the transnational corporations have not been able to organize the world to their liking in secrecy and with no opposition.[9] One hopes they will not be able to do it at all.

For centuries, the structures and institutions representing the international elite class have had a huge investment in hierarchy, competition, and divide-and-conquer tactics. They put vast resources into keeping the world the way they want it. They prefer to do it quietly, or even invisibly, but, if necessary, they will use the influence they have over our governments. Governments, in turn, use such forces as their armies, intelligence services, media, police, schools, and weapons to maintain control of the population.[10]

A world of systems designed to preserve injustice and inequality is held in place by several interrelated expressions of "power-over:" political power, economic power, physical force, and ideological power.

Political power works by putting only members of a certain group in positions where they can make decisions affecting the general population. In North America, we have mainly white, straight (or perceived as straight), upper-class and upper-middle-class males making decisions that affect vast numbers of people. Political power tends to concentrate in fewer and fewer hands, because those who make the decisions favour their own group, giving themselves increasing power.

Economic power—where one group has access to more economic resources than others—tends to concentrate in the same way. The favoured class uses its resources to further increase its wealth and, with that, its economic power. In Canada in 1973 the richest 10 percent of families earned 21 times the income of the poorest 10 percent. By 1996, the richest 10 percent were earning 314 times the income of the poorest 10 percent (Yalnizyan 1998). The gap was widened by a quarter-century of public-policy decisions heavily influenced by the wealthiest citizens.[11] The way they use their spending power, along with their political power, affects millions of other people's lives.

Political and economic forms of power are backed up by the power of physical force. Large corporations, drug cartels, and governments can back up their control over others through action or threat of action by security forces, thugs, and armies.

There is another form of power that makes the previous three possible. This is ideological power, the power of belief. It is ideological power that allows an individual or group to influence others' concepts of reality and their idea of what is possible and valuable. If people believe that injustice and inequality are right, or at least inevitable, they will not try to change their society. This silence and inaction becomes the ballast that steadies the whole system. It creates an appearance of peace and order; people's discouragement about the possibility of changing the *status quo* keeps the current power relationships in place without obvious force having to be used.[12]

Some specific beliefs that prop up injustice are:

- the myth of scarcity—the belief that there is not enough to go around, frequently used to disguise the fact that a large proportion of the world's resources benefit very few people. For example, the richest 20 percent of the world's population make 86 percent of consumer purchases, use 58 percent of the world's energy, and create 53 percent of the world's carbon dioxide emissions, while the poorest 20 percent make 1.3 percent of consumer purchases, use less than 4 percent of the world's energy, and create 3 percent of the world's carbon dioxide emissions (United Nations Development Program 1998:2–4). One person living in the United States consumes a hundred times as much of the world's resources as a citizen of one of the poorest countries (Arnfield undated), and causes a hundred times the environmental damage (umanoski 1990). A North American uses energy equal to that used by 3 Japanese, 6 Mexicans, 14 Chinese, 38 Indians, 168 Bangladeshis, and 531 Ethiopians (New Roadmap Foundation 1993). The average annual pocket money for a child living in the U.S. is $230, more than the annual income of half a billion of the world's poorest people (Durning 1992:153). The world's resources are adequate to give everyone a good quality of life. The problem is domination of resources by a few powerful people. In other words, the problem is the inequalities of class.
- the myth of objective information—the belief that it is possible for one group, particularly straight white males in this part of the world, to stand back and observe humanity without their own biases influencing what they see;
- stereotyping—the belief that all members of a group are the same;
- blaming the victim—the belief that people are responsible for their own oppression. An example is the strong tendency in North American culture to blame a woman for being raped, beaten, or harassed. The first questions asked are what was she wearing, what did she do, and what kind of a woman is she, as if she brought the violence down on her own head. Another example is the assumption that poor people

are "lazy." When many people believe that the poor are to blame for their own misfortune, attention is directed away from the real causes of poverty.[13] This attitude is internalized by the poor themselves, who then tend to live in shame and hostility towards other members of their own group;

- might is right, or "majority rule" in situations where only a small minority are really calling the shots. The majority can be threatened, manipulated, bought, or given only the appearance of choice;
- separation, competition, and hierarchy—the belief that human beings are isolated individuals in competition with one another for positions on a ladder of status.

These beliefs are maintained by:

- tokenism—one member of an oppressed group is given a high-status position and then used as an example which validates blaming other members of that group for not "making it" like that person did;
- assimilation—absorbing marginalized cultures into the dominant one;
- private ownership of information;
- private ownership of the means to communicate information. Those who hold political and economic power also own radio and television stations, newspapers, publishing houses, and magazines. In Canada the information media is in the hands of eleven corporations, six of them controlled entirely or almost entirely by one person. In 1970, a Special Senate Committee on Mass Media was concerned that the three biggest newspaper chains controlled 45 percent of circulation when they had controlled only 25 percent in 1958. By the time the Kent Royal Commission on Newspapers reported in 1980, these three chains controlled 57 percent. Now they control 72 percent. Ordinary people are constantly exposed to the version of the truth carried by these information media, a version of the truth acceptable, in the long run, to the owners of the media. David Radler of Hollinger Inc., owner of 151 newspapers, has said: "I don't audit each newspaper's editorial each day, but if it should come to a matter of principle, I am ultimately the publisher of all these papers, and if editors disagree with us, they should disagree when they're no longer in our employ. The buck stops with the ownership."[14]
- violence or the threat of violence. Oppression is held in place ultimately by violence in its many forms—visible, such as injury and death, or less visible, like exclusion, denial of access, and denial of

needs. Violence prefers not to show its face. Whenever possible, oppression is held in place by the fear of violence.

Anyone involved in social justice activism sees this fear all the time. People often do not fight for what they need and see as right because of this pervasive fear of reprisal. When you ask people to sign a petition on the sidewalk, many look at you with fear in their eyes and back away. When the possibility of a march or demonstration arises in a group, people tend to immediately think of reasons why they should not do it.

There is political repression in Canada, although most of it is hidden from sight and excluded from history texts. Miners and other unionists have been shot on picket lines (Abella 1974, Allen 1973, Calhoun 1983, Kuyek 1990:17–25, and Mellor 1983). People's leaders and organizers have been imprisoned (Salutin 1980). Tear gas, pepper spray, and police horses disperse demonstrations. Guns have been hidden in leaders' houses to be found again when the police come to search.[15] Telephones are tapped and files kept. Opponents of uranium mining have been harassed by helicopters flying repeatedly over their houses.[16] Groups have been infiltrated. Activists have been intimidated, bribed, and threatened with release of private information until they agree to become informants (Fidler 1978, Mann, Lee and Penner 1979, Sawatski 1980). Many, many social change activists, even those who simply begin to speak up a little for themselves, experience a backlash from members of the oppressor group. Gay and lesbian activists receive anonymous threats of death or rape. Such terrifying calls and notes also plague feminist, First Nations, and Black activists who gain the public's attention.[17] Those who try to change oppressive relationships on an individual level can experience violence as well. For example, women who try to change unequal relationships with their male partners sometimes receive verbal, psychological, or physical violence in response.

Those who speak up against injustice or immoral uses of power are more likely to experience indirect reprisals than outright physical violence. They may lose their livelihood, become painfully isolated, have their reputation smeared, or be branded as "troublemakers." For example, four scientists working for Health Canada experienced "persistent harassment by management, including conspiracy, threats, intimidation, and defamation" after pointing out gaps in the study used to prove the safety of Bovine Growth Hormone, a genetically altered hormone injected into dairy cattle to increase their milk production.[18] Two journalists in the United States were fired for producing a documentary including some of the same questions about Bovine Growth Hormone raised by the Canadian scientists.[19] Other labels, like "socially maladjusted," carry with them the threat of institutionalization for psychiatric "care" (Blackbridge and Gilhooly 1985).

Canada is not Guatemala or Turkey. We do not face the extreme repression carried on in many other parts of the world. However, a little violence goes a long way here. An occasional, unpredictable display of repression can make an average, law-abiding citizen refuse to sign a petition. This is the principle of terrorism. For every person hurt, a thousand more are persuaded not to rock the boat. Direct, violent repression is always there, in the background, but for us in Canada, it is more important to understand fear and the other quiet, invisible, self-perpetuating methods of control the elite classes have established.

One could argue that Canada is a very advanced example of invisible oppression. Our government is quietly handing our country to our current colonial masters, the United States, wrapped and tied up with a bow.[20] Our international reputation continues to shine in spite of the terrible things we have done to nations and peoples less powerful than ourselves.[21] Our national reputation continues to glow with innocent goodwill in spite of the gross inequalities we live with every day.[22] We continue to write off the violence we practise systematically against each other as aberrant individual cases.[23] Groups working towards alternatives are so dependent on government funding that they feel they have to compete with one another whenever a bit of funding is dangled in front of them. We seem to have a national case of wearing rose-coloured glasses.

We must overcome these methods of control if we are to take the first steps toward unity, equality, justice, and a humane culture—a culture with a future.

Notes

1. Analysis of the transnational corporations and their strategies can be found in the work of Sarah Anderson (2000), Maude Barlow (1990, 1998; and Heather-jane Robertson 1994; and Bruce Campbell 1991, 1996; and Tony Clarke 1997a, 1997b, 1998a, 1998b, 2001), Susan George (1976, 1979, 1984, 1988, 1992, 1999; and Fabrizio Sabelli 1994), Brewster Kneen (1993), Jerry Mander (1991, 1996), Linda McQuaig (1987, 1991, 1993, 1995, 1998), Maria Mies (1986, 1993), Jan Nederveen Pieterse (2000), Boyce Richardson (1997), and Vandana Shiva (1993, 1997, 1999, 2001; and Maria Mies 1993), to name a few. There are also good resources on the Internet, including CorpWatch [http://www.corpwatch.org], The Council of Canadians [http://www.canadians.org], The Ecumenical Coalition for Economic Justice [http:/

/www.ecej.org], Focus on Global Trade [http://www.focusweb.org], Susan George's Home Page [http://www.tni.org/george/index.htm], The International Labour Organization [http://www.itcilo.it/english/actrav/telearn/global/ilo/multinat/multinat.htm], MAI? No Thanks! [http://www.geocities.com/athens/3565/], MAI-Not [http://mai.flora.org], The Multinational Monitor [http://www.essential.org/monitor/index.htm], NDP on Trade and Globalization [http://www.ndpontrade.parl.gc.ca/resources.htm], The New Internationalist Magazine [http://www.oneworld.org/ni/index4.html], Ratical.Org [http://www.ratical.org/corporations], the Sierra Club [http://www.sierraclub.org, http://www.sierraclub.ca/national], Third World Resurgence [http://www.twnside.org.sg], and many others.

2. This quote is in a letter from Alexa McDonough and Svend Robinson of the New Democratic Party Federal Caucus on the "NDP on Trade and Globalization" website [http://www.ndpontrade.parl.gc.ca/dear_activist percent20letter.htm].

3. Coverage of the Summit of the Americas and the demonstrations in Québec City can be found in any Canadian news source for April 16–22, 2001. See also *RESIST! a grassroots collection of stories, poetry, photos and analyses from Québec City and beyond*, complied by Jen Chang et al., 2001, Fernwood Publishing, Halifax, NS.

4. CBC National Radio News, 8:00 a.m., April 23, 2001.

5. See note #6.

6. These cases are listed on the "NDP on Trade and Globalization" website listed in note #1. Another source of information on these cases and others is Swenarchuk (1999).

7. There is information on these protests on the Internet sites listed in note #1. Also see any news source at the time of these meetings.

8. See the MAI? No Thanks! and MAI-Not websites listed in note #1.

9. See note #8.

10. There are thousands of examples of governments practising repression in the interests of multinational corporations. Many are included in the books and websites listed in note #1 above. Three classics on the subject are Pearce (1982), Petras and Morris (1975), and Plant (1978). See also the reports of the American Friends Service Committee, including Yarrow (1999) and American Friends Service Committee Office of Curriculum Support—School District of Philadelphia (1999).

11. A detailed account of how this process works can be found in McQuaig (1987).

12. Ideological power was first defined and explored by Antonio Gramsci (1988). For a chilling example of the use of ideological power in apartheid South Africa, see Lambley (1980:12–36, 159–223). Maria Mies gives a detailed example of the use of ideological power to keep oppressed people in place in "The Myth of Catching-up Development," in Mies and Shiva (1993:55–69, 124–27).

13. An excellent analysis of "poor-bashing" can be found in Swanson (2001a).

14. This information on the Canadian media, along with the quote from David Radler, comes from the website of the Campaign for Press and Broadcasting Freedom [http://www.presscampaign.org/ownership2001.html and http://www.presscampaign.org/circulationdata.html]. Other good sources of information on this issue are Friends of Canadian Broadcasting [http://friendscb.ca], the Canadian Media Awareness Network [http://www.media-awareness.ca/eng/issues/mediaown/mediaown.htm]. Equivalent websites for other countries include: Columbia Journalism Review (U.S.) [http://www.cjr.org/owners], Australia [http://www.comslaw.org.au/research/Ownership/index.htm], Europe [http://elj.warwick.ac.uk/jilt/commsreg/97_3doyl/default.htm], U.K. [http://www.cultsock.ndirect.co.uk/MUHome/cshtml/media/mediaown.html], and The Global Media Giants (international) [http://www.fair.org/extra/9711/gmg.html]. Also see Kuyek (1990:26–31), and Winter and Hassanpour (1994).

15. This is from a speech by Georges Erasmus, telling the story of resistance to the proposed Mackenzie Valley Natural Gas Pipeline, at a workshop called "North and South: What's the Connection?" sponsored by Project North, held at the Centre for Christian Studies, Toronto, March 1975.

16. Experience of friends involved in lobbying for the ban on uranium mining in Nova Scotia, 1981–82.

17. Personal experience and first-hand accounts from friends.

18. The scientists were Shiv Chopra, Mark Feeley, Gerard Lambert, and Thea Mueller. Their story can be found on the website of the Sierra Club of Canada [http://www.sierraclub.ca/national/genetic/bghback.htm]. It was also told in a documentary produced and aired by CBC's investigative journalism program *The Fifth Estate* in November 1994.

19. The two journalists were Jane Akre and Steve Wilson. There is information on their case on [http://www.foxBGHsuit.com].

20. This is a reference to Canada's support of U.S. positions in international trade agreements and our participation in U.S. military actions such as the Persian Gulf War in 1991, the on-going embargo of Iran, and the NATO bombing in Kosovo.

21. Canada's record abroad is far from glowing. Two classics on this topic are Carty and Smith (1981) and Swift and Clarke (1982). More recent information can be found on the Probe International website [http://www.probeinternational.org/pi/index.cfm]. Part of the goal of this website is to "expose the environmental, social, and economic effects of Canada's aid and trade abroad." Other sources of information are Sanders (1996) and the National Film Board of Canada/Alter-Cine film *Hand of God, Hand of the Devil* (1996).

22. Every year, the United Nations Development Program surveys a number of countries—from 160 in 1991 to 174 in 2000—according to its Human Development Index. The Index measures life expectancy, literacy, school

enrolment, gross domestic product, education, status of women, children, aboriginal people, and senior citizens, and poverty rates. Every year from 1994 to 2000 Canada was named the best country to live in, despite getting poor marks on the gap between rich and poor, the poverty rate for children, gender equality, human rights, and treatment of aboriginal peoples. Canada had the second widest income gap in the "developed world." See Thompson (1997) and Leopold (2000). The governments of Canada and Ontario have used the report extensively in their advertising, to the point that the 2000 Report warns both governments against complacency (Leopold 2000). Linda McQuaig makes an analysis of this study and its use in Canadian Government advertising (1993:97–119).

Canada has the second largest gap between rich and poor among developed countries, after the United States. For example, in 1999, the richest 10 percent of families had a median net worth of $703,500, while the poorest 10 percent were in debt by $2,100. In that year, the amount of personal wealth in Canada had grown by 11 percent since 1984, but the poorest 20 percent of families had lost an average of $600 in assets. The richest 20 percent had increased their net worth by 39 percent, or about $112,300 (Statistics Canada 2001). This study may not tell the whole story. It was based on 16,000 responding households, so probably did not include Canada's wealthiest families, like Ken Thompson with $20 billion in assets, or Canada's poorest families, such as those on First Nations reserves, in military camps, or in hospitals and nursing homes (Swanson 2001). For more information on Canada's growing gap between rich and poor, see McQuaig (1987), Statistics Canada and Lars Osberg (1981), Oja (1987), Yalnizyan (1998), and the Basic Income website [http://www.basicincome.com/basic_candata.htm].

23. For an excellent example of attributing systematic violence to aberrant individuals, look for Canadian press coverage of the murder of fourteen women in Montréal, December 6, 1989, and the subsequent anniversaries of that occurrence. Examples are McGillivray (1990), Lalonde (1991), and Conlogue (1991).

Morality, Duty, and Being True to Yourself

We admire people who oppose the regime in a totalitarian country and think they have courage or a 'strong moral sense' or have remained 'true to their principles' or the like. We may also smile at their *naïveté*, thinking, 'Don't they realize that their words are of no use at all against this oppressive power? That they will have to pay dearly for their protest?'

Yet it is possible that both those who admire and those who scorn these protesters are missing the real point: individuals who refuse to adapt to a totalitarian regime are not doing so out of a sense of duty or because of *naïveté* but because they cannot help but be true to themselves....

Morality and performance of duty are artificial measures that become necessary when something essential is lacking. The more successfully a person was denied access to his or her feelings in childhood, the larger the arsenal of intellectual weapons and the supply of moral prostheses has to be, because morality and a sense of duty are not sources of strength or fruitful soil for genuine affection. Blood does not flow in artificial limbs; they are for sale and can serve many masters. What was considered good yesterday can—depending on the decree of government or party—be considered evil and corrupt today, and vice versa. But those who have spontaneous feelings can only be themselves. They have no other choice if they want to remain true to themselves. Rejection, ostracism, loss of love and name calling will not fail to affect them; they will suffer as a result and will dread them, but once they have found their authentic self they will not want to lose it. And when they sense that something is being demanded of them to which their whole being says no, they cannot do it. They simply cannot.
—Alice Miller (1983:84–85)

Chapter Four

Step 1: Understanding Oppression—
The personal is political

> The problem, unstated til now, is how
> to live in a damaged body
> in a world where pain is meant to be gagged
> uncured   ungrieved-over   The problem is
> to connect, without hysteria, the pain
> of any one's body with the pain of the body's world
> —Adrienne Rich (1986)

Twice in my life I have been part of experiments in cooperative group functioning that I would call completely successful. One was a workplace, the other a voluntary group. Both practised collegiality, consensus decision making, cooperative planning, shared work, a negotiated division of tasks, personal support, and opportunities for learning—for a time. Neither lasted more than two years. Both broke up quickly, completely, dramatically and, for me, painfully.

My current work sometimes involves mediating conflicts in voluntary organizations. I see the patterns of my own painful experiences repeated over and over again. Sometimes I feel I am watching the same play performed by different theatre companies.

The pattern is this: after months of muttering outside of the decision-making forum, a person or small group suddenly tries to establish control, sometimes directly, but more often through hidden, manipulative means. While attempting to take control, they express feelings of being persecuted or unsafe. They often believe that someone is trying to take control of them, and sometimes they seem even to be unconscious of the steps they are taking to gain control. They challenge whomever they perceive to be in a position of leadership. If the challenge is accepted by the person or people challenged, or by someone else, a power struggle follows. Once a power struggle begins, anything goes—backroom organizing, running to get support from someone who is perceived to have power over the situation, dramatic performances, lies.

In the end, it seems, the only option is to destroy the whole experiment, or at least its spirit, since the cooperative spirit cannot be controlled and survive. As with a consensus-based culture trying to resist conquest by a competitive one, once the battle for control begins, "power-over" tactics must be resisted by using "power-over" tactics. The prerequisites for "power-with"—openness, trust, vulnerability, creativity, risk, emotional expression, honesty, giving before receiving—become impractical. Anyone who tries to maintain these ways of interacting is bound to lose what is now structured as a win-lose battle and perhaps be injured in the process.

During these incidents, everyone involved experiences extreme confusion, pain, and a sense that the real problem is underlying and unspoken. The surface expression of the disagreement seems shallow, completely irrational, or shifts quickly among several different points of disagreement. Consensus becomes impossible. People are forced to take sides. The tension is personalized—people cease to like, trust or cooperate with one another. Above all, the depth of emotion, distrust, and the sense of danger go far beyond any actual threat present in the group. The power of the feelings in such a situation is amazing; people are passionate about the stands they take, even while unclear exactly what their stands are.

Where do these dramatic, emotional group disintegrations come from? Why do people who have so much in common do this to one another? Why do the best of our cooperative experiments seem to explode with the greatest intensity? How does the practice of "power-over" become so deeply ingrained that even those of us who have committed our lives to finding different ways of being together fall back into it so completely?[1]

The first time I was part of a story like this from beginning to end, I was in the midst of the experience when I received a clue. A friend took part in a workshop on counselling adult survivors of childhood abuse. When she told me about it, she listed symptoms that may indicate childhood abuse. The list included sharp intelligence, watchfulness, competitiveness, well-developed skills in manipulating people, and a strong need to control every situation. I began to wonder about the person who was trying to control our situation. Later, after all was said and done, it turned out that she was indeed a survivor of incest. Her awareness of her past had been emerging during our conflict.

This led me to ponder a possible connection between child sexual abuse and some adults' need to exert control over others. After all, such a connection would have huge implications for our efforts to change power relationships. Childhood sexual abuse is not uncommon. About a third of the hundreds of women I know as friends, associates, and acquaintances, all over the world and across many races and cultures, have at some time told me about their memories of childhood sexual abuse.

Although there are no national statistics on child abuse in Canada, we are gradually becoming more aware of the extent of child abuse as the issue receives more public attention. Most of the attention has been focused on sexual abuse. Although it is now seventeen years old, the most extensive study of child sexual abuse in Canada is still the 1984 Committee on Sexual Offences Against Children and Youths (The Badgley Committee). It concluded that:

- one out of two females (53%) and one out of three males (31%) in Canada have been victims of at least one unwanted sexual act;
- four out of five of these are committed when the victim is a child or youth;
- four out of one hundred young females have been raped;
- two in one hundred young people have experienced unwanted anal penetration;
- three out of five sexually abused children were threatened or physically coerced;
- one out of four assailants is a family member; one out of five is the child's father; one out of two is a friend or acquaintance (Badgley 1988).

A 1991 report, *Foundations for the Future*, says that 9 percent of girls and 12 percent of boys under the age of seven in Canada are repeatedly sexually abused; 37 percent of girls and 36 percent of boys under the age of twelve in Canada are repeatedly sexually abused (Health and Welfare Canada 1991). In 1991, *Canadian Living Magazine* reported that sexual abuse directly affects between 75 percent and 95 percent of Canadian families (Kaye 1991).[2]

Even these figures may be underestimations, as the power to commit sexual abuse also includes the power to silence the victims with threats, shame, and a strong sense of family privacy. According to David Finkelhor, in *Sexually Victimized Children* (1979), 63 percent of abused girls and 73 percent of abused boys who reported their abuse as adults did not tell anyone while they were children. Many also bury the memory in their subconscious. The memory may resurface in later years, sometimes not until old age.

I began to watch similar situations and to look for literature on the connection between childhood abuse and a need to control others. I found very little. Most writing on child sexual abuse is concerned with how adult survivors function emotionally and sexually and in intimate relationships. Few articles look at survivors' use of power as adults.[3]

My personal observations told me that there is some connection between child sexual abuse and a need to control situations later in life, but there is not a consistent pattern. Of the dozens of women I know who experienced sexual abuse as children, I have seen only a few abuse power in groups. On the other hand, I have seen some abuse power who, as far as I know, did not experience sexual abuse as children.

Then I clicked. I had been swept away by the drama and perhaps even the pornographic aspects of sexual abuse, as the news media so often is. The key is not the sexual nature of the abuse, but the child's experience of powerlessness. Children's experience of powerlessness at the hands of adults is so common, world-wide, that it passes for "normal."

Adult power over children is unavoidable. It is used to protect children and maintain their well-being. It can be accompanied with explanations, negotiation, and fair demands made on everyone in the household, young and old. It can be limited to protecting the child's health and well-being, while the child's own decisions are supported in situations where the consequences are not as serious. Adult power must be used to fill the needs of children. All too often, it is used to fill the needs of the adults, and child rearing becomes centred on obedience instead of child development. Obedience works best when a child has low self-esteem and is discouraged from thinking for her or himself.

When programs are introduced in schools to help children learn to value themselves and think independently, a significant number of parents actively resist. For example, in 1987, Timberline Press in Eugene, Oregon, developed a dragon puppet called Pumsy, with accompanying lessons to be used by teachers and guidance counsellors. The objective of the program is to help children think clearly, increase their confidence, and respect others. The exercises involve children in such activities as visualizing saying "no" to a drug dealer or discussing what they would do if they found twenty dollars. Pumsy was used in 16,000 United States schools and was challenged by parents in eight states in 1992 alone. According to the Halifax *Daily News*, most of the objections criticized the lessons that help children learn decision-making. The parents were upset because the dragon "undermines parental authority" and "contradicts Christian beliefs that only parents, or a higher power, have the right to tell children how to act" (Halifax *Daily News* 1993).[4]

Fortunately, Pumsy seemed to be winning many of these battles, but the parental objections demonstrate the commonly held understanding that children should think of themselves as lesser beings and as under their parents' authority in all things. This belief, along with the experience of being raised this way, encourages adults to keep children in a state of anxiety, to undermine their self-esteem, and to stress unquestioning obedience. This collection of conditions is often referred to as emotional abuse. Sometimes children are intentionally treated this way; more often it is a reflection of the adults' own state of anxiety, low self-esteem, and training in obedience.

Almost all North American children grow up experiencing some form of emotional abuse. Alice Miller's series of three books, *For Your Own Good* (1983), *Prisoners of Childhood* (1981), and *Thou Shalt Not Be Aware* (1986), explores the cruelty and humiliation hidden in some of the most commonly held beliefs about child rearing in Western culture.[5] She also examines how abusive methods of controlling children—methods designed to break a child's will rather than develop a child's awareness and skills—are perpetuated, generation after generation. The isolation, shame, and secrecy of the patriarchal nuclear family help ensure that abusive child-raising methods are passed down through families, without examination.

Even when children experience no abuse from parents or family, they experience pain and powerlessness in other settings. Anyone who spends time in Native communities or communities made up of Third World people, sees children everywhere. They often have a voice in family and community decision-making and participate in every community event, playing on the floor when they get bored, falling asleep in a corner when they get tired. No one is bothered by their noise and activity. A babysitter is very rare.

Western culture, on the other hand, does not place much value on children's opinions or welcome them as part of adult activities. When a child cries in a supermarket or public lecture, the parent tries urgently to shush them while other adults cast annoyed glances in their direction. Margaret Green, a white South African Jewish psychotherapist working in England, says: "Try as a parent to let your child carry on crying on a bus or pee in a public place or even try breastfeeding beyond the first year or two. You will be criticized, ridiculed, and made to feel extremely isolated. Our culture has institutionalized the oppression of children" (1987:207).[6]

Children also experience pain and powerlessness when they encounter the oppressions that are the subject of this book—racism, poverty, and discrimination based on disability, learning style, language, geographic location, religion, and gender. Some children have families who help them understand and deal with the pain and injustice of oppression; others are not so lucky. Some children's families can help them learn survival tactics; some cannot because the family does not share the oppression. This is often the case when the child's oppression results from a disability, a bisexual, gay, or lesbian sexual orientation, or a transgendered identity. Sometimes when other family members do not share the oppression, they contribute to the child's experience of powerlessness by rejecting, patronizing, overprotecting, or trying to change the child.

The severity of adult power abuse varies greatly. It can range from comments that make a child feel self-conscious to treatment that could be called torture. Also, different people carry childhood abuse into adulthood in different ways and to different degrees. There seems to be little correspondence between the adult reaction and the severity of the abuse if, indeed, severity can be judged. What most North American children carry with them into adult life, however, are the fear and low self-esteem that come from experiences of powerlessness and the strategies they learn for self-protection.

What are the strategies children learn to protect themselves from powerlessness? They learn to be afraid, to distrust, to be watchful, and to make clear distinctions between "us" and "them," safe and dangerous. They learn that they are part of a hierarchy based on deception and force. They learn to judge the situation and make the choice that faces all people who lack power—whether to go along with the situation, run away, or fight.

When they decide to go along with the situation, they obey, conform, and stay silent. Children learn to cozy up to those who can hurt them, say what the adults want them to say, please and protect adults, act on their behalf, disguise their own intelligence and power, and pretend to take pleasure in their own abuse. They learn to be afraid of what power they do have; they learn to deny it and see themselves as even more powerless than they really are. They also blame themselves for the situation and thereby reduce their self-esteem.

When children decide to fight back, they sometimes learn to take every opportunity to grab a little power for themselves and use it to the limit. They can develop a large repertoire of methods for manipulating, controlling, and disempowering others, even for destroying them. Abuse survival, whatever form it takes, requires great intelligence and skill.

Survival also requires the suppression of feelings—emotion can make a person with too little power even more vulnerable. Even in situations where abuse is not involved, emotional expression is heavily discouraged in North American anglophone culture. A society structured around competition for control of others requires the control of self, for both the controller and the controlled. Alice Miller writes that denial of emotions separates people from their deep moral sense and therefore makes people obedient and "adaptable," that is, capable of being used for anything. Part of Miller's explanation of this phenomenon is included as a quote at the beginning of this chapter (Miller 1983:83–85). This relates closely to the process of making men into soldiers, discussed in Chapter Two. Emotion, like sexuality, must be crushed to make a man able to fight and kill.

An African friend once arrived at a meeting feeling shaken. She had been walking along a Toronto sidewalk and passed through a group of people. Afterwards, she realized that she had just walked through a group emerging from a funeral parlor. She was shocked because of the disrespect she had just shown the mourners and also because she could not tell they were mourners! There was no crying, no wailing, no expression of grief at all. Her comment was: "No wonder North Americans can be controlled so easily!" At the time I did not understand what she meant; now I do.

Expressing one's emotions is healing and liberating. When a person is physically wounded, bleeding prevents infection or, if infection has already taken place, the wound gathers pus that must be released for healing to take place. Likewise, tears release pain, shouting and physical movement release anger, shaking releases fear, talking and laughing release a variety of tensions, conversation and physical touch communicate loving support between human beings. All these are necessary for emotional healing to take place.[7] When emotions are released, they can be seen and shared, and others who have experienced the same feelings can offer support. This can begin the process of collective healing as well, for the first step is to discover that we are not alone, not imagining it, not to blame, and there is no reason for shame. Every time someone breaks through the bounds of shame—the "privacy" taught by our dominant culture—others flock to them saying, "Yes, that happened to me too." By repressing physical and emotional expression, the culture we live in blocks individual healing and the possibility of people uniting around shared pain.

Because emotional healing is often denied, either by the adults in a family or the general culture or both, a child experiencing powerlessness must deal with the pain in some other way. It is sometimes buried somewhere in the unconscious mind. Many adults who were abused as children have no memory of the experience. Memories may emerge, usually as flashbacks, later in life, sometimes when the person is middle-aged or older. Until then, healing or even conscious reflection cannot be initiated, but the pain is still there, affecting the person's reactions to new situations. Unhealed childhood pain seems to be a key mechanism for learning how to behave as oppressors and oppressed. Childhood scars leave a deep distrust of the possibility of safety and equality, and many of us as adults react by using and accepting "power-over," by creating hierarchies wherever we go.

Margaret Green has made a very direct connection, not just between unhealed childhood pain and unconscious oppressive attitudes in general, but between the experience of a particular oppressive attitude and its later expression. The context of her experience is her leadership of "unlearning racism" classes for white women. She says: "The most interesting feature of emotional work on being racist is that hardly anyone ever sticks to the topic ... if one attempts to work with any one of [the participants] they will invariably revert to the hurts related to their own oppression" (1987:193). "From the emotional work done in these [workshops], it becomes evident that experiences of oppression in early childhood provide the fertile ground in which the unconscious roots of racism develop and are allowed to flourish. The common factor linking the many and varied experiences of oppression is the conscious and unconscious abuse of power in relation to children" (179).

For example, she describes women searching for the source of their fear of asking questions about other cultures. They find it in childhood memories of what seemed to them adults' bizarre behaviour in the presence of people of colour. A woman remembered her grandmother telling her that people were black because they were covered with chocolate. Another was told out of the blue that a black man standing nearby was no different than she was and she should remember that. As children, these women knew the information was untrue, and when they questioned further, the adult became upset and dragged them away. The memories were painful because it was clear that they were lied to by someone they loved and then silenced when they tried to figure it out. They experienced powerlessness in the face of something that didn't make sense.

Another participant lived in a mixed-race neighbourhood and enjoyed it until she had a baby of her own. She then became frightened of the Black people in her neighbourhood and worried about her baby's safety. She wanted to move away and yet felt guilty because she knew that her attitudes were racist. Work on her memories and feelings brought back a childhood incident where her grandmother had read her a story about

Black people in Africa being cannibals and eating white babies. This information had frightened her at the time but was later repressed along with the memory of its source.

Another example involved a woman who was short-tempered with Black women who attended a clinic where she worked. As she explored her feelings, it emerged that she was upset at the number of children they had while she had been trying to conceive for over a year. This experience connected with early messages about Black women's fertility.

A woman found it difficult to be warm and welcoming with the male immigrants who came to the advice centre where she worked. As she explored the roots of this reaction, she uncovered her experience of being unwelcome in her own family.

Green says:

> It is the internalization of our personal experiences of oppression which perhaps cause us to feel inadequate, ugly, ridiculous, invalidated, objectified, fearful or terrified. If these experiences remain unresolved, we then project on to the external world. Who or what we perceive as embodying a threat to our existence, be it personal, social or economic, is very much determined by institutionalized prejudice and prevailing myths and stereotypes which serve to manipulate and fuel our fears. (1987:196–97)

How exactly does it work? How does the pain of childhood powerlessness become adult abuse of power or acceptance of abuse, adult oppression or acceptance of oppression? This is a question that has intrigued many researchers, scholars, philosophers, and writers, particularly those who have survived times and places of obvious cruelty, such as Germany under Hitler or Latin America under U.S. domination. From among many various explanations, I have found five that make sense to me.

The first I found in Re-evaluation Counselling, a program I participated in, on and off, for ten years. Although it originated with Harvey Jackins, Re-evaluation Counselling theory has been built by the collective thinking of hundreds of re-evaluation counsellors who communicate through the various journals that serve as their network.[8] According to this theory, unhealed pain is like a gully carved in our thinking. Each time we see a situation that looks anything like the one that hurt us, we do not stop to think creatively, we simply react with whatever behaviour might protect us, whatever behaviour protected us in the past. In this way, childhood survival tactics are used automatically and irrationally by adults who have more power in their current circumstances and could react more creatively. The situation itself may be similar to the original hurtful situation in only one respect. Suddenly, however, it is as if the person is back in the situation of abuse—hurting, frightened, and powerless in the face of someone with much more power. The old survival skills click into action: judge the situation, distrust everyone, go along with what is happening, denying what power you do have, or fight back by manipulating and controlling.

Sometimes survivors whose childhood pain has never been allowed to heal will abuse a less powerful person if their survival reaction has been triggered by the belief that their victim has power over them. For example, men who batter their partners often see their action as controlling a person who will hurt them if they do not strike first.[9]

Margaret Green points out that some roles in society institutionalize this cycle.

> Teachers will say how they never intended to treat children "that way." But they find themselves shouting, for example, or about to use violence. They may begin to see themselves pitted against the children rather than as the allies and collaborators they had always intended to be. Of course, there is hardly anyone alive today who has not experienced some form of mistreatment at school. Being in the position of teacher sanctions the re-enactment of childhood hurts. There are for instance schools where corporal punishment is still allowed. If that is the case, then lesser everyday crimes like invalidation, ridicule and humiliation, and the suppression of creativity will surely go unnoticed. (1987:207)

A second theory on how childhood pain becomes adult abuse of power can be found in Alice Miller's work. She uses a Freudian theory, "splitting and projection," to explain the mechanism (Miller 1983:79–91). According to her analysis, abused children split off the parts of themselves they have learned to hate, particularly their weak, powerless child-state. Later, as adults, they project these hated parts of themselves onto children, or others less powerful than themselves, and then punish the children, or others, for their own feelings of helplessness. This theory could explain why we so often direct our power against members of our own oppressed group. If we have suffered because we are women, or First Nations, or gay/lesbian, or Black, or because we have a disability, we may split off that feared and hated characteristic of ourselves. Later we may direct our fear and hatred at whoever exhibits those parts of our identity, particularly if they are proud of it.

A third explanation can be found in the writings of several therapists who work with adult survivors of child abuse. They document a tendency of adult survivors of abuse to distrust and severely test, even abuse, any person or group that expresses love towards them. This reaction comes from low self-esteem—the feeling that one could never be worthy of kindness, love, and support.[10]

A fourth explanation comes from the work of Arno Gruen. He believes that when children experience pain from their parents, they adapt by dissociation; that is, they split their interior and exterior worlds apart. They see their parents as the parents see themselves—loving, kind, good—and suppress their own perceptions of their parents, as a source of pain. They lose consciousness of their own inner life, particularly their feelings of helplessness and can only play the roles expected of them by those more powerful than themselves. They create the illusion that they share adults' power by obeying and pleasing them. When they grow up they can become destructive, abusive people because they have lost empathy with others, along with all their other feelings, are terrified of powerlessness, and suffer from self-hatred—a result of betraying themselves and submitting their will to others. (Gruen seems to feel that children choose to submit. To my mind, children are too dependent to choose; however, it seems very common for adults to believe that they chose to submit to abusive treatment as children). In this dissociated state, people can be manipulated by those willing to take power over them, and they can feel alive and safe only when they take power over others. They believe, however, that their destructive "power-over" is love, just as they were taught to believe that their parents' power over them was love. With no feelings, no inner life, they cannot tell the difference (Gruen 1987).

A fifth explanation is that the pain of extreme loss of control, unhealed, becomes the source of extreme fear of loss of control. Adults who carry this fear with them seek control in every situation in order to feel safe (Laidlaw, Malmo and Associates 1990:46).

The five psychological mechanisms described here—adult use of childhood survival skills, splitting and projection, distrust of good treatment, dissociation, and extreme fear of loss of control—help me understand why members of groups who seem to have everything in common and have operated cooperatively for some time can be triggered by something that brings controlling behaviour into play and destroy the group. The unhealed pain from past experience of powerlessness, buried in individuals, builds the intensity of these battles.

So many experiments have been based on creating a community based on similarities, all-lesbian communities for example. The point is to leave behind the conflicts arising from diversity. The problem is, participants in such communities still take their scars along with them. Within a short time unhealed injuries from past experiences have the group tearing each other apart. The community, based on similarity, experiences all the same struggles as the most diverse of coalitions.

Because we all carry the roles of both oppressor and oppressed very deeply rooted in us, it becomes very difficult for alternative ways of functioning to gain a foothold. Cooperation, equality, consensus, negotiation, and power sharing are constantly sabotaged by fear and the beliefs about reality sealed into our old scars.

I am not suggesting that we should blame individuals who break down experiments in cooperation because of their childhood scars. Rather, I am looking for the mechanisms that cause us all to reproduce oppression generation after generation in Western society. These mechanisms are obviously complex and may vary from culture to culture. My analysis is, of course, limited by such factors as my class, gender, colour, ideology, and location in the world.

The phenomenon I have observed of an oppressed individual becoming an oppressor may also work on the collective level. I remember my surprise when I first learned that during the Anglo-Boer War, the Afrikaners were the ones who were oppressed. They faced the well-equipped professional army of the British with rag-tag guerrilla bands, while much of their population died of hunger in concentration camps and their farmland was laid waste.[11] I had thought of them only as the people whose government developed the oppressive system of apartheid in South Africa. I wondered why their humiliation and defeat seemed to give them, or rather their leaders, a determination to oppress others, instead of sympathy for those trying to resist oppression and scrape a livelihood from the land. How can a safe, prosperous, independent homeland be achieved by the methods they have used? Their logic is that of an unhealed survivor.

Abuse is sometimes used deliberately to teach children to fit into the system of oppression when they become adults. Two examples of this are boarding schools for upper-class young men and Indian residential schools. In the case of boarding schools for upper-class young men, the boys are separated from their families, particularly their mothers, at a very young age. The lessons of repressed emotion, hierarchy, competition, and obedience are reinforced constantly. Above all, in many of these schools there is a tradition of "hazing," or the "fag" system as it is called in the U.K. Older students are encouraged to torment and abuse younger students. In school, then, young boys first experience oppression, then later are in a position to oppress others.[12] This is excellent training for young men who will some-day hold power in industry, government, the justice system, and the education system. They are being trained to wield power and authority in the very institutions that maintain the oppressive *status quo*. Margaret Green calls this system

> the perfect training ground for the colonial administrator who would be expected to treat his Third World underling with similar contempt. The role provides the opportunity, and the person filling it experiences enhanced social status, a sense of self-worth which contradicts his early experience, and at the same time a release of tension which accompanies the re-enactment of a hurt in a position of greater power. (1987:207)

The second example, Indian residential schools, is one of child abuse being used to force a people to internalize what their conquerors thought to be their rightful place in a racist, sexist, class-stratified society. Stories are emerging now from across Canada that describe the physical, emotional, and sexual abuse that First Nations children suffered in these schools.[13] In Chapter Two, I included a long quote discussing the ideas of Father Paul LeJeune, a missionary to the Innu people in the sixteenth century. Even that early, LeJeune saw clearly that in order to teach First Nations people the hierarchy, competitiveness, and violence of Europe's dominant cul-tures, they would have to take Native children away from their communi-ties and abuse them.

At first glance it may seem strange that the same methods have been used with the intention of training both oppressor and oppressed, upper-class men and First Nations people. This fact illustrates that oppression is a single system, in which most of us play both roles. Learning to reproduce that system is a single process. Margaret Green says: "If one imagines a person on a see-saw alternating between the two possibilities, oppressor and victim, then emotional work on either role undermines the fulcrum and eventually the whole structure will collapse" (1987:195).

Many children who have experienced the pain of powerlessness with inadequate opportunity to heal survive by learning to use a variety of tactics. If they feel they can control the situation, they do so; if control is impossible, they learn to protect themselves by obeying and pleasing, or they undermine others. In other words, they learn that they have a place, with some people more powerful than they are, some less. They learn hierarchy and its forms of power well—not consciously but as a pattern in their deepest survival instincts.

Upper-class men are supposed to learn not only to oppress others but also respect and obey those above them in the hierarchy. The intention with First Nations people, as well, was for them to learn both subservience to whites and oppression of their own people. In both cases, they learned to maintain the structures of oppression, no matter where they fit into them at any given time. Paula Gunn Allen observes this logic in Father LeJeune's journal: "How could they understand tyranny and respect it unless they wielded it upon each other and experienced it at each other's hands? He was most distressed that the 'Savages,' as he termed them, thought physical abuse a terrible crime" (Allen 1986:39).

Unfortunately, many of us raised in our abusive society can understand no other forms of power besides power over another or another's power over us. We carry within us a blueprint of the culture's oppressive patterns to be reproduced wherever we have influence. The name for this is "internalized oppression." Thus, the ways of "power-over" follow their cycle from macrocosm to microcosm and back again. We, as individuals, are the DNA of our cultural patterns of misused power. "Power-over" is self-perpetuating. The personal is indeed political.[14]

Notes

1. A very interesting book has been inspired by infighting among lesbians, examining the ethics and values that prevent us from working together. See Hoagland (1988).
2. Up-to-date information on child abuse for Canada can be found on the web site of the National Clearinghouse on Family Violence at [http://www.hc-sc.gc.ca/hppb/familyviolence/index.html], and other relevant information can be found on the Department of Justice information page on child abuse at [http://www.extension.ualberta.ca/legalfaqs/nat/v-chi-en.htm]. For U.S. statistics, information and research, see the National Clearinghouse on Child Abuse and Neglect Information at [http://www.calib.com/uccanch]. In the U.K. the only national source of statistics is a series of joint studies done by National Statistics and the Department of Health. These can be ordered at [http://www.doh.gov.uk/public/hpssspub.htm]. Another excellent source of information is the About.com web page on child abuse at [http://incestabuse.miningco.com/health/incestabuse/cs/childabuse/index.htm]. Most of the material on this web page comes from the U.S., but there is international information as well. For more information on incest, see Butler (1978).
3. I have found the following research articles that make some connection

between childhood abuse and a need to control others: Brickman (1984:49–67, 1992:128–139), Courtois and Sprei (1988:270–308), Johnson (1988:405–28), and Laidlaw, Malmo and Associates (1990:46). A strong connection is made between authoritarian, male-dominant homes and incest, and the implications for the perpetuation of these power structures in families and society are discussed in Asher (1988).

4. Gloria Steinem tells a story of right-wing reaction against self-esteem programming similar to the parental resistance against Pumsy. The programs were carried out by the California Task Force to Promote Self Esteem, and measurable positive results were achieved in a very short time in schools, prisons, women's and youth centres. However, the final report was greeted by anger, and an attempt to reproduce the Task Force on a national level was defeated by right-wing forces that saw an increase in self-esteem as dangerous for obedience to God and legitimate authority. See Steinem (1992:26–33).

5. Also see Chapter Two, note #4, Rose (1991), and Starhawk (1987:206–7).

6. Vandana Shiva discusses the exclusion of children from the Western development model in "The Impoverishment of the Environment: Women and Children Last," in Mies and Shiva (1993:70–88).

7. My comments on the healing power of emotional expression and the patterns that result from unhealed pain come from my ten years of involvement with the Re-evaluation Counselling community. Much of my understanding of oppression generally also comes from this experience, although it is impossible to disentangle my experience with co-counselling from the many other experiences I have had with oppression. One of the strengths of Re-evaluation Counselling is its understanding of the collective nature of oppression and its effects on the individual. The community and its various caucus groups (Black, Jewish, Women, etc.) publish excellent newsletters full of insights into the nature of oppression. For further information on this system of counselling, see: Jackins (1973) and Personal Counsellors Inc (1962). The organization is based at Personal Counsellors Inc., Box 2081, Main P.O. Station, Seattle, Washington, 98111, U.S. Their website can be found at [http://www.rc.org]. A more theoretical discussion of healing through emotional expression can be found in Scheff (1979).

8. See note #7.

9. For further explanation of batterers' perception that their female partners have more power than they do, see: Canadian Advisory Council on the Status of Women (1987).

10. Low self-esteem is mentioned in virtually every book and article about childhood abuse survivors. The specific problem of being unable to accept good treatment is discussed in: Brickman (1992:128–39), Cahill, Llewelyn and Pearson (1991:117–30), Courtois (1988: 98–99), Courtois and Sprei (1988:270–308) and Laidlaw, Malmo and Associates (1990:178).

11. I made this discovery about the history of the Afrikaner people in Harrison (1981), Michener (1980), and Sparks (1990), particularly Chapter Six, "The

Great Trek Inward" (119–46), and Chapter Seven, "The Rise of Apartheid" (147–82). Information on the concentration camps can be found on-line at the website of the Anglo-Boer War Museum in Blomfontein, South Africa, and that of the Boer Nation. See [http://www.anglo-boer.co.za/concent.htm] and [http://www.boer.co.za/boerwar/weber.htm].

12. I learned what I know of life in upper-class boy's boarding schools from conversations with friends who had the experience and from occasional news reports of hazing incidents that have gone too far. The only discussion I have seen in book form is in Leemon (1972).

13. There is a rapidly growing body of literature on the Indian residential schools. See Brooks (1991:12), Bull (1991:Supplement), Campbell (1991:28), Ing (1991:Supplement), Knockwood (1992), Lill (1991), Milloy (1999), and the Royal Commission on Aboriginal Peoples (1996).

14. "The personal is political" was one of the key early insights of feminism. Our foremothers saw the division of life into "home" and "world," "private" and "public," with women assigned to one, men to the other, as one of the foundation stones of women's oppression.

A Story: Racism and Sexism

This interaction of racism and sexism took place at a weekend workshop designed to introduce a group of white Canadians to some aspects of First Nations culture. The event arranged for the first evening was a Sweat Ceremony, led by a respected Elder. We traveled to the Reserve and spent the day visiting sites of ceremonies and communal gatherings, asking questions, and listening to stories told by the Elder who was our host. We watched a group of young men prepare the Sweat Lodge for our ceremony later in the day.

Evening came. We were divided into gender groups and told that the women would go first. We had a briefing from the young men assisting the Elder. One member of our group had not yet decided to go through the experience with us. She confessed to occasional experiences of claustrophobia and wanted to know if she would be allowed to leave if she began to feel panic. The young men assured her that she could, so she decided to go ahead with it.

Once inside the Sweat Lodge, she did begin to feel claustrophobic. We were seated in a circle around a pit filled with scalding rocks. The air was close and filled with the incense of burning cedar. The moment arrived when the tarpaulin was to be pulled down over the door. Our friend decided that she could not stand to be closed in after all. She asked if she could leave before the tarpaulin was closed. The Elder, who was seated between her and the door, said no. She panicked, rose to her feet, and tried to scramble past him through the still open doorway. The Elder rose too and pushed her back into her place. She tried to escape again and again was forced back to her seat. The rest of us asked him to let her go and continue with the rest of us. He refused and offered us lessons, telling us that white people are weak and soft, undisciplined, and divorced from the earth.

I agreed with much of what he said. By then, however, all of us felt trapped by the tarpaulins and afraid. Our fears of male violence had been aroused, instilled in us by our own culture and experiences. It was a relief when he said he wanted nothing more to do with us and told us to get out of his Sweat Lodge. The men's sweat ceremony followed. They had a good experience.

The next morning we rejoined the First Nations members of our workshop to discuss our experience in the Sweat Lodge the night before. It was an angry, tense session. We tried to explain how we, as women, felt trapped by male violence. Even many of the White men did not understand what we were trying to say about our disempowerment as women. The First Nations people explained to us the absolute respect they have for their Elders and their long, painful experience of white people despising their culture. To them, once again, a group of white people had shown disrespect to a leader of their community, a wise man held in great esteem.

I have learned that the interaction between racism and sexism is always very complex, and many of us barely learn to grasp one reality. It has taken me years to even begin to understand what they may have been saying. One piece fell into place when a friend told me of another unsuccessful introduction of a group of white people to a Sweat Ceremony. The Elder in her situation had explained that the Sweat Ceremony, like many other spiritual rituals in the Native tradition, is meant to be an initiation or trial. The purpose is to persist through the discomfort and pain and by doing so pass to a new spiritual level. When white people (or anyone else) go through the experience for recreation, fun, or because it is "interesting," we are not taking the spirit of the ceremony seriously. We bring with us our assumption that pain and discomfort are abnormal and something to be "gotten rid of," something to be ended quickly by popping a pill. We are missing the point, taking the role of uninvolved observers, and taking an important part of Native culture very lightly. This is indeed the spirit in which we had entered upon our experience of the Sweat Ceremony.

Another possible clue was a statement by another Native Elder about his discomfort with white women. He confessed that his first memory was of being beaten by a white woman, a nun at the Residential School. If the Elder who had led our Sweat Ceremony had similar memories, no wonder our actions were disrespectful and threatening to him.

At the workshop where this sweat ceremony took place, we did not succeed in reaching a common understanding where we could all feel heard and respected. Everyone had come to the weekend intending to work at overcoming our long history of oppression, but the remainder of the workshop was marked by distrust and anger. Unfortunately, we did not part as friends. Even if the experience had been positive, perhaps it was unrealistic to expect that hundreds of years of oppression and lifetimes of conditioning could be changed in a weekend.

Chapter Five

Step 2: Understanding Different Oppressions

If only it were possible to draw a line through humanity with The Oppressor on one side and The Oppressed on the other—for example, Capitalists on one side, Workers on the other—liberation would be so much simpler. But it does not work like that. There are probably a few people in the world, members of the international elite, who fall almost completely on the oppressor side. There are also some who are almost entirely oppressed; for example, street children in cities of the South.[1] The vast majority of us, however, belong somewhere in between; we are oppressors in some parts of our identity and oppressed in others.

As long as separation, hierarchy, and competition are the underlying assumptions, this interweaving of power roles helps keep the whole system in place. For example, imagine an anglophone, heterosexual, white woman with a disability who sits on the board of her family's multinational corporation and an able-bodied professional Black man who is gay and has a first language understood by only a few thousand people. If both of these individuals wish to maintain their own sense of superiority, they each have several reasons to look down on the other. If they become aware of their oppression and desire to move towards liberation, they can each claim that the other is their oppressor. In the process, they reinforce their own oppression by maintaining the cycle of hierarchy and competition. It would take a long time and a great deal of work for them to ever become allies. Only a complete and complex understanding of their own contradictory roles as oppressors and oppressed would allow them to recognize their shared interests.

To begin an analysis of ourselves as oppressor and oppressed, it is important to give some thought to the differences and similarities among the forms of oppression we experience.

Differences

Visible and invisible

There seems to be a cycle of envy between visible and invisible oppressed groups. The visible resent the ability of the invisible to blend in with the mainstream for purposes of getting jobs, housing, education, and all the other advantages normally reserved for the more privileged. The invisible envy the greater progress that is made on visible oppression issues because the presence and size of a visible oppressed group cannot be ignored. Also, the invisible envy visible minority people because they can find each other in order to organize and see each other in order not to feel alone in a room. These points of envy create an unfortunate and damaging division between oppressed people.

This division appears within the ranks of those who are struggling on issues of disability because some physical differences are visible, and others are not. The visible suffer the immediate discrimination of people who become uncomfortable in their presence, treat them as children, or ignore them altogether; the invisible must continually make decisions about who to tell, when, and why. They do not get the sympathy for their cause that those with the more visible disabilities receive.

Another example is the tension between gay and lesbian people and visible minority communities. When I travel or eat in a restaurant with visible minority friends, I am grateful that I am not visible. Some racist incident, small or large, happens at least every half-hour. It is harder for them to see some of the things faced by those subject to an invisible form of oppression like heterosexism; for example, the insulting comments people sometimes make because they assume everyone present is heterosexual, the damage done to our self-worth when we hide or lie to cover up our sexual orientation, or the fear that we will be separated from our partners in the event of injury or illness.

The issue of visibility/invisibility invites us to play "my oppression is worse than yours." It is an issue that deserves attention for the sake of everyone's liberation.

Specific histories of peoples

The form that oppression takes is affected greatly by the particular history of the group in question. Compare the oppression of Jewish people to that of Deaf people. The identity of Jewish people has taken shape through a history of being forced to leave one country after another. Jewish members of the Re-evaluation Counseling community have written about the imprint this history has left on them, collectively and individually. They say it is difficult for them to feel welcome anywhere.[2]

According to the Deaf individuals I know or whose work I have read, their oppression revolves around the accessibility of communication and the legacy of poor literacy and education from lack of communication, mistreatment of deaf children, and the misdiagnosis of deaf children as mentally challenged.[3] Such different specific sources of oppression are bound to shape the struggles of these two peoples differently. They will be hurt by different things, aim their efforts at different problems, and fight different institutions, to the point where they may not even recognize each other as potential allies in fighting oppression.

Sometimes different histories cause hostility between people experiencing different forms of oppression. For example, many African-Nova Scotians attest to the importance of the Christian tradition to their survival and the acceptance they find in their church communities.[4] Part of the teaching of that tradition, however, is that gay and lesbian people are sinful and an "abomination." Ironically, the word "abomination" has racist roots. It refers to the practices of another culture and religion that are despised and considered inferior by one's own culture and religion.[5] Most gay and lesbian people have had a negative history with Christianity. Various churches have strongly supported our oppression—sometimes our destruction—since the Inquisition.[6] Sometimes the result of these different historical relations to Christianity results in tension between the Black community and gay and lesbian people and a painful rift in the lives of some gay/lesbian people who are Black.

Aboriginal/non-Aboriginal groups

The particular nature of Aboriginal rights can sometimes create tensions between First Nations people and others involved in various human rights struggles. Aboriginal people in Canada, like Aboriginal people everywhere, have a special connection with and certain rights to their land, in this case the North American continent, that other groups do not have. The Aboriginal struggle is not only for the resources, protection, and respect they deserve as human beings and as peoples, that is, basic human rights, individual and collective. It is also a struggle to recover their nationhood and their right to their homelands, that is, their Aboriginal rights.[7] Aboriginal people still need human rights; the people of a First Nation can suffer under their own leadership as well as under foreign domination. However, the tendency of many people to throw the struggle of Aboriginal people in with all other human rights struggles disregards the unique nature of Aboriginal rights and leads some Aboriginal activists to separate themselves from other human rights issues.

For example, I have seen exchanges on more than one occasion between African-Nova Scotians who want to include people in anti-racist activities and Mi'kmaw people who do not want to be involved. The Blacks want the two groups to take a unified stand against racism, a human rights issue, but the Mi'kmaq[8] do not want the common cause of racism to disguise the differences between the two groups over the issue of Aboriginal rights.

Class and Other Forms of Oppression

Class is the layering of our society into different levels according to how much access people have to wealth and power. When we speak of the "high," "upper," or "elite" classes, we mean people who control a great deal of wealth and power. When we speak of the "lower" classes, we mean people who are poor and vulnerable to decisions made by others. In some ways class is similar to other forms of oppression, but in another very important way it is unique. The similarity or difference depends on whether you are looking at the cultural aspects of class or its political and

Class and Other Forms of Oppression

Diagonal Oppressions: Racism, Sexism, Heterosexism,
Discrimination based on Disability, National Origin, Religion, etc.

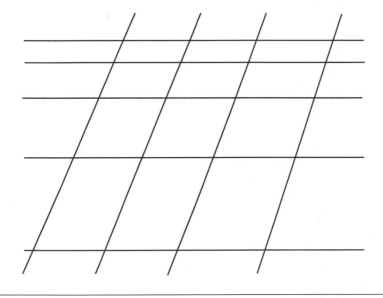

Class

economic aspects. Class has both, and we must deal with both in our social justice work.

When class is considered as a cultural phenomenon, it affects relationships among individual people in the same way that other oppressions do: there is inequality and there are degrees of privilege; the privileges are for the most part invisible to those who have them. It is very difficult, but not impossible, for good-willed and conscious people in the more privileged levels of the class hierarchy to become allies of those with less. In a cultural sense, class is an idea or perception, just like the other oppressions. In other words, there are strengths and weaknesses, advantages and disadvantages for those of different classes. A working class person can appreciate not being as naive as some professional people, or someone who grew up in a "middle class" family can be happy that they were not separated from their parents like many "upper" class children who grew up in nurseries, summer camps, and boarding schools. In a purely cultural sense, it is only because society says that "upper" class is better than "lower" class that one is often experienced as better than the other.

In the same way, white is not better than Black, male better than female, nor heterosexual better than gay or lesbian. The unequal values assigned to these differences are also ideas and perceptions. When we work to change these cultural oppressions, many of our tactics are ideological or cultural. They are aimed at ending shame and developing pride in those who have internalized the understanding that they have a lower value than another group. When the issue is class, it is also important to deal with the cultural aspect and fight peoples' sense of shame over being poor.

However, on a structural level, class is different from other forms of oppression such as racism, ageism, and sexism. Class is not just a factor in inequalities of wealth, privilege, and power; it *is* that inequality. Other forms of oppression help keep the hierarchy of power in place; class is that hierarchy. Class is the beginning point and end product of all other forms of oppression. It is the essential structure of society, the sum total of all the other inequalities.

I sometimes explain the relationship between class and other forms of oppression by drawing a series of horizontal lines on a piece of paper, then a series of diagonal lines cutting across the horizontal lines. The horizontal lines represent class; the diagonal ones represent other forms of oppression. Other oppressions, such as racism, for example, cut across all classes, but the lower you go in class levels, the more people of colour you will find. Racism affects all people of colour, no matter what their class, but it will affect those in the higher classes less than those in the lower classes, because those with wealth and power can use their resources to ease the impact of racism on their lives.

Another example is disability. You will find more people with disabilities the lower you go in the class strata, because discrimination based on disability affects the education and employment opportunities of people with disabilities. Also, a disability limits the life of a person in a lower class more than it does someone who has more wealth and power. The person with more wealth and power can use the resources available to overcome the barriers they face. Such a person could buy a van equipped with a wheelchair lift, for example, or hire a sign-language interpreter for a lecture he or she wants to attend.

Racism, discrimination based on disability, and the other "diagonal oppressions" are causes and effects of the class system, and they help hold it in place. For example, when people's time is taken up by the struggle to survive or make ends meet, it is difficult to take part in the kind of reflection that makes one aware of inequalities and the structures that cause and perpetuate them.

A second example is the process of scapegoating. When low-income tenants complain that the landlord collects their rent and doesn't keep up their buildings, they will often focus on the fact that the landlord is white or Jewish, for example, rather than the fact that the landlord-tenant relationship is one of class. People will blame their economic troubles on the language or religion of the better-off part of the population instead of their class. Middle-class people will blame low-income people for their poverty because of their colour or because they are women, instead of seeing the class structure that actually causes their poverty. It is so much less risky to blame the vulnerable rather than the powerful. These reactions reinforce class inequality by taking attention away from it and blaming the suffering it causes on some other difference instead.

When we are fighting the other forms of oppression, sooner or later we come up against class, because sooner or later we must address the real lack of power and resources faced by people forced to bear the stigma of other oppressions. This is usually the point where we hit real resistance, as well. Those who already have wealth and power in our society are often ready to accept a change of attitude but not our attempts to redistribute wealth.

When we fight class inequalities, we are not just trying to change attitudes. We are trying to change people's access to resources, their real voice in political decision making. As one of my friends says, "When we fight racism, the purpose is not to make people white; when we fight sexism the point is not to turn women into men; but when we fight poverty, the purpose is to get people out of poverty."[9]

Likewise, we can conduct many fights against other forms of oppression with few resources, because ideological strategies depend more on creativity, sharp analysis, and people's readiness to take risks and express themselves. When we reach the point of challenging class, the struggle itself requires resources—either funding or some other alternative—because the people involved do not have the resources to carry on the fight. Even basic things like getting to meetings or finding someone to care for children while adults talk are out of reach when poverty is the issue or a significant part of the issue.

These differences illustrate the unique aspect of class as a form of oppression. Class is a political and economic structure as well as an ideological one. The other oppressions are building tools; class is the wall. The other oppressions are cause and effect; class is the resulting structure. The other oppressions make it possible for some people to justify having access to the resources of others; class is the fact that they have that access. We must deal with the cultural aspects of class, but class is not just another form of oppression.[10]

Similarities Among All Forms of Oppression

Power and hierarchy

The basic common denominator among different forms of oppression is power and hierarchy; that is, class. One group of people believes they are superior over another and can back it up with "power-over." The "power-over" can come from physical strength, weapons, greater wealth, resources, or information, or greater control of the decision-making and communication mechanisms of the society. These means allow the oppressor group to control the oppressed group and help themselves to the less powerful group's resources. They can also effectively spread the idea that the less powerful group is inferior. Both groups internalize this hierarchical thinking and begin to act it out through the mechanisms described in Chapter Four. Power-over and hierarchy are fundamental components of all oppressions. They constitute the basic class structure in which all other forms of oppression operate.

Stereotyping

Stereotyping is tricky because it does not come out of the blue. Stereotypes are usually built on a real observation of a culture, just as prejudices often evolve from a kernel of truth. A comment that is a damaging stereotype in one situation, from one person, can be a compliment somewhere else, from someone else.

For example, in North America Jewish mothers have been at the centre of some cruel humour that combines sexism and anti-Semitism to portray a large group as simple-minded, overbearing, and possessive. This group contains millions of scientists, carpenters, artists, deep spirits, great minds, loving women, women with a sense of humour, women struggling with addictions, peacemakers—name it, you will probably find it among Jewish mothers, along with every conceivable variety of child rearing beliefs and skills. All of these women, however, are pushed into one limited, insulting picture. That is the damage of stereotypes.

On the other hand, some of the humour about Jewish mothers can be taken as appreciation for the love, care, and concern that many women give to their children in the generally highly valued family structure of the Jewish community. What makes the difference is the relationship between the person making the comment and the Jewish mother who is the object of the humour, along with the exact audience, content, tone, implications, and words.[11]

I am not suggesting that an absolute judgement can be made on whether a given remark, story, joke, or portrayal is a damaging stereotype or an affectionate, supportive one. The person speaking may have the best intentions and catch the recipients at a point in their struggle where the remark is hurtful. If twenty people hear the comments, there will probably be twenty different reactions on a scale between damage and compliment. Even in a small group where people are well known to one another, you cannot count on a stereotype being received exactly as you intend.

It is very difficult to avoid stereotypes. They seem to be present all the time, almost a form of conversational shorthand. However, even though stereotypes are almost unavoidable and can be positive, they are most often used in a damaging way against marginalized groups. Many have suffered and died because negative images of their people were established in the institutions with the power to imprison, kill, forcibly hospitalize, take jobs and homes away, and separate people who love one another.

Stereotyping is part of the concept of separation. It divides people into "us" and "them." A dominant group sees itself as a collection of different individuals and a marginalized group as a single collective entity. I am writing these words a few days after terrorists destroyed the World Trade Centre in New York City and part of the Pentagon in Arlington, Virginia. According to the news media, there is reason to believe this attack was carried out by an organization based in an Islamic state. The news is full of the phrase "Islamic militants," painting several governments, millions of people, and a major world religion with the same brush. The U.S. President stated that his country's retaliation "will make no distinction between the terrorists responsible and those who shelter them."[12] If the U.S. finds a government guilty of sheltering terrorists, this threat extends also to the millions of innocent people who live in that country. On the other hand, when Timothy McVeigh was convicted of bombing the Federal Building in Oklahoma City in 1995, no one referred to him as a "Christian militant." No one threatened to make war on the state or city where he lived. He was universally portrayed as an evil or deranged individual.

All groups are stereotyped to some degree, but those with power cannot be hurt by them as much as those with less power. Although the specific characteristics are different, all oppressed groups are undermined by damaging stereotypes.

The structure of violence

All oppressed groups encounter the mechanisms institutions use to keep us "in our place" when we step out of it. We experience harassment, withdrawal of resources, slurs against our reputations, denial of promotion (or good grades, service, or housing) for sketchy reasons. Some members of oppressor groups use violence to maintain their superiority. These tactics include threatening letters and phone calls, beatings, graffiti, vandalism, and sometimes even murder or terrorism as a message to others who are thinking of standing up for their rights. There is little outcry when such tactics are used against oppressed groups, compared to the public disapproval expressed when they are used against the privileged.

Oppressed groups also share the less obvious tactics used by people with power, such as tokenism, claims of liberal equality ("we're all equal now; you are asking for special rights") or funding competition (oppressed groups are forced to fight over artificially limited resources).

Assumptions/slurs concerning sexuality

In my experience, every oppressed group has been assigned at least one false negative belief related to sexuality, usually the belief that the oppressed group is out of control or immoral sexually: "Black men want to rape white women," "Black women are sexier," "Indian women are a good lay and cannot say no," "People with a disability have no sexuality," "People with a mental disability are out of control and must be institutionalized;" "Lower class people breed like rabbits;" "Gays are immoral;" "All women want to be raped," and so on.[13] White South Africans held under house arrest for their anti-apartheid activities have reported receiving letters from conservative South African whites accusing them of all sorts of unacceptable sexual practices (Paton 1982). Their "crime" is their opposition to racism; but their tormentors immediately interpret it sexually, just as women who want more independence from their husbands are often accused of having an affair with another man.

The connection between sexuality, particularly women's sexuality, and racism emerges again and again. In the anti-racism workshops I co-led, we would ask people to list words and phrases which contain "black" or "dark" and "white" or "light" (Bishop and Carvery 1994). We always got a mixture of expressions with a primarily racist history, such as "the black sheep of the family," and those with a primarily sexist history, such as "black witch" or "black cat." In *Women of Crisis II* by Robert Coles and Jane Hallowell Coles, a Native woman is quoted: "I'll never forget the nurse telling me that Indians are dark and we get our 'periods' before they do, the Anglos ... [Indian] children ... started bleeding early, because they are dark" (Coles and Coles 1990). Darkness and femaleness are linked in their portrayal as chaotic, fearful, and evil.

I think this close connection between sexuality and various forms of oppression demonstrates the importance of sexuality to the spiritual and physical well being of humankind and comes from the time when men began to take the control of their people's destinies away from women.[14] The ideas and values used to subjugate the female are applied to both women and men of marginalized groups—we are all seen as being closer to the earth and the animals and are, therefore, lower, more bound up with our bodies and sexuality—evil, seducing, insatiable, and destructive. Women and marginalized groups are also accused of being sexually violent, although in reality it is the dominant group that more often acts out sexual violence.

I find it very interesting that there is at least one sexual myth about every oppressed group. I think it shows how strongly straight white men equate controlling another person with controlling his or her sexuality. Do they believe that control of sexuality gives them control over future generations? Or perhaps this belief comes from the history of oppression, because the first human beings to use "power-over" were probably men subjugating the women of their own people.

Assumptions concerning treatment of and access to children, and efforts to separate the oppressed from children, even their own

I was amazed long ago to read a piece of historical fiction about the relationship between the Jewish and Roma (Gypsy) peoples in Europe during the years leading up to the Second World War, a relationship that grew from many years of shared marginalization. Unfortunately I have long since forgotten exactly what book it was, but one particular point stayed in my mind—both Roma and Jewish people were accused of stealing and abusing children. It startled me because it is so similar to the accusations made against gay men, lesbians, and witches. At that point I began to watch for myths concerning oppressed groups and child abuse. I found many.

They divide into several types of myths. The first are the extreme ones—the oppressed group steals children, eats them, uses them as slave labour, sacrifices them in rituals, or abuses them sexually. Once again, here is the oppressor group scapegoating marginalized groups, for it is the oppressor who steals the children of the oppressed group for slavery, both physical and sexual. The same false accusations also appear in a more subtle form. For example, "women sexually abuse children as often as men do," or "gay men and lesbians recruit children." These myths turn up constantly in the media and in any meeting or radio phone-in show discussing child abuse.

Yet a third form of this myth has to do with people's ability to bring up their own children. Young boys are removed from their mother's care to become "men" in boarding schools; the children of indigenous people all over the world are placed in boarding schools run by the oppressor;[15] some charities that care for poor children offer no health care, nutrition, education, or employment support to their parents[16]; for many years Black and First Nations children were placed in white adoptive homes when families in their own communities wanted them;[17] and social welfare systems take children from their natural parent and give them to higher-class foster parents who are paid a daily allowance several times the amount of the social assistance paid to the natural parent.[18]

A fourth form has to do with the ideological rather than the physical separation of parents and children. The children of oppressed people are subject to constant messages, in school and the media, that their parents are not to be respected or emulated. Children of oppressed people are encouraged to despise their parents and scorn their parent's ancestry, history, dignity, and struggles, in the interests of teaching them to identify only with their oppressors. Later, when some members of an oppressed group begin to speak out about their experience, others counteract their messages, speaking out in favour of the oppressor group whose perspective they have internalized.

For example, many Native people in Canada are currently speaking out about the abuse they experienced in the residential schools. In response, others are contacting the public media to say that these stories are exaggerated or completely untrue.[19] If the latter group were saying only, "my experience did not include abuse," they would not necessarily be speaking out of their internalized oppression. When, however, they try to silence and deny the experience being expressed by others of their own people, they are acting on behalf of the oppressor, whose interests they internalized long ago.

One way a dominant group can attempt to control an oppressed people's future is by controlling the education and development of their children. Going one step further, they can even try to control the oppressed group's bearing of children. An example is the massive and expensive efforts right-wing groups make to control children at the fetal stage. Their attempts to take decisions about childbearing out of women's hands cause pain and hardship for many women. The logic of their actions seems to be that the interests of women are opposed to those of children. However, the real welfare of future children is tied up intimately with that of women; only a group that is trying to take ownership of children away from their mothers could think that inflicting suffering on women is in children's best interests.[20]

In addition to the physical creation and ownership of the child, the oppressor must also be concerned with what influences the child's belief system, that is, with ownership of the process of creating the adult from the child. The more the bearing and raising of their own children can be removed from the oppressed group, the more chance the oppressor group has of making a society in its own image and to its own advantage and keeping it that way.

Desire to separate and distinguish
The more the oppressor group can separate and distinguish itself from the oppressed group, the greater is its capacity to create and carry out policy, take possession of resources, and build an ideology of oppression—all part of taking and maintaining control. The oppressed group has to make a choice, and most are split over it. If they decrease the separation and distinctions, they have a better chance of getting in on the privileges and resources reserved for the oppressor group. If they are involved in a process

of liberation, playing down distinctions helps them focus on commonalities with other oppressed people. On the other hand, the more they can separate and distinguish themselves, the more chance they have of preserving an identity and spirit that will allow them to survive their oppression and move as a group towards liberation.

Specific similarities
There are also particular similarities between some forms of oppression. For example, there is a specific similarity between Deaf people and gay/lesbian people. Both groups have a collective identity and culture that is not learned in the individual's family of origin. An estimated 95 percent of deaf children are born and raised in hearing families; more than 90 percent of gay/lesbian children are born and raised in heterosexual families. This situation often leaves scars on the individuals of both groups, as many have to break with their family to find positive role models and must struggle to build their self-esteem and counter the negative self-images they received as children. Both cultures have difficulty being recognized as cultures because they are not passed from parents to children, but unite people that are no blood relation.

Distinctions Within the Major Oppressions

The process of understanding the relationships among different forms of oppression is complicated by the fact that there are many different expressions of the major forms of oppression. These different expressions can become sources of competition or at least distrust. For example, in Nova Scotia the history and form of racism directed towards the Black population is different from its expression towards the Mi'kmaw First Nations people. The slavery and broken promises that brought Black people here, killing thousands, was the result of racism. The appropriation of land and resources that pushed the Mi'kmaw people onto tiny, inadequate reserves, killing thousands, was also the result of racism. The two histories, however, were different.

As a result, the current generation of Black and Mi'kmaw people apparently have different aspirations. The stated aim of most Nova Scotian Black organizations is a fair share of the resources controlled by white society, integration, and an end to distinctions based on colour. On the other hand, most Mi'kmaw organizations say they aspire to sovereignty based on their Aboriginal right to the land that was theirs. Sovereignty means even clearer distinctions and the right to discriminate on the basis of time spent occupying the continent. Both groups recognize the power of racism, and sometimes they can make common cause, but sometimes they cannot. Sometimes they react against one another because of cultural differences or because of their frustration with constantly being thrown together as visible minorities in programs that cannot fill the different needs of both groups.

Another example of variations in the same oppression can be found in the different ways heterosexism is experienced by gay men and lesbians. Because heterosexism is part of sexism, it affects men and women differently. Heterosexism as it applies to men is about five thousand years old. As described in Chapter Two, male-dominant, war-oriented societies use heterosexism to reinforce male ownership of women, male superiority to women, and the relationship men require with one another in battle. Sexuality in such societies is related as much to conquest and ownership as it is to pleasure, so intercourse between men means that a man is conquered, possessed, lowered to the status of a woman. If he chooses this status, he insults the superiority of the male. Much can be achieved in shaping men for a war-making culture by encouraging hatred of those men who love other men. The literature of patriarchal peoples is full of heterosexism in reference to men.

Today, this legacy results in several expressions of heterosexism directed specifically at men. One is the fear that young men, forming their masculine identity, feel towards gay men and act out in "gay bashing." Another is the variety of responses gay men have to women. Some cherish their "feminine" side and develop a deep understanding of and friendship with women; some develop a hatred of women beyond that of straight men; some find self-expression in women's clothes, or "drag," although it is not uncommon for "drag queens" to express great hostility towards women.

On the other hand, there are very few references to women loving women in patriarchal literature before this century. This is because, until this century, most women in patriarchal societies have been considered possessions of men and therefore have had even less choice of sexual expression than gay men had. Lesbians suffered this lack of choice along with other women, and many feel oppressed by sexism as much as by heterosexism. Some of that sexism we experience from our gay brothers.

The concept of the lesbian only emerged during the early part of this century, as women began to develop independent lives and careers and therefore gain some space to express their sexual choices (Faderman 1981). Heterosexism as it is directed against lesbians is often indistinguishable from society's general resistance to women's independence. Men who batter their partners sometimes accuse them of being lesbians, simply because they have shown some resistance to male control of their lives. Women who take leadership in feminist organizations tend to be called lesbians for the same reason, no matter what their sexual orientation. Many people in this society make no distinction between a lesbian and a feminist.

The oppression of lesbians grows directly out of our history as women in patriarchal societies, and results in heterosexism taking a very different shape for us than it has for gay men. Our reactions, therefore, are sometimes not only different from theirs but in complete opposition. Hence the struggles inside gay/lesbian organizations over issues like pornography and women-only space. Lesbians also resent having research and analysis of gay men automatically applied to us. Our community, culture, and issues are often different from those of gay men.

The same type of situation occurs with discrimination based on disability. The experience of society's stigma is very different for someone in a wheelchair than it is for someone who has chronic pain. It is difficult to form an organization to defend the rights of all people with disabilities when the language of the Deaf must be visual and the language of the blind must be oral. It is difficult to build trust when Deaf people have a history of being perceived as mentally challenged and, consequently, some Deaf people want to distance themselves from those with a mental disability.

The picture is extremely complicated! There are many points where marginalized peoples can work against each other and compete with each other. Those in power are always ready to foster these divisions and reap the benefits. If we are going to be able to build the kind of solidarity that can change our society, we will have to be very clear on the different forms oppression can take, and look through them to see our common interests.

Notes

1. For more information on street children, Human Rights Watch has a paper on their website called "Promises Broken: An Assessment of Children's Rights on the 10th Anniversary of the Convention on the Rights of the Child" (December 1999) [http://www.hrw.org/campaigns/crp/promises/index.html]. They also have a basic information page on street children: [http://www.hrw.org/children/street.htm]. Other good resources are Castilho (1995) and the World Health Organization (1993).

2. For more information on Re-evaluation Counselling and its caucus groups, see Chapter Four, note #7. For more information on Jewish history, see the large collection of Jewish history texts at the Internet History Sourcebooks

Project [http://www.fordham.edu/halsall/jewish/jewishsbook.html].

3. For more information on Deaf culture and community, see American Library Association (1992), Benderly (1980), Gannon (1981), Goldstein (1989), Greenberg (1970), Jacobs (1980), Kannapell (1980), Padden (1980, 1988), Sacks (1990), and the large collection of texts at [http://deafness.about.com/health/deafness].

4. For more information on the role of the church in the survival and development of the Nova Scotia Black community see Henry (1973:122), Pachai (1987:50–52), Walker (1980:32–33, 42–43, 54, 107–108, 135–40), Winks (1971:53–58, 138–39, 339–51, and the text collections linked to the website "Gateway to Black Nova Scotian Resources" [http://www.library.dal.ca/ssh/gateway.html].

5. The word translated as "abomination" is the Hebrew "to'evah" or "to'ebah." It means "ritually unclean" or "idolatry" and refers to the rituals of religions other than Judaism. It carries a strongly judgmental connotation, therefore establishing a hierarchy of peoples and contributing to racism. See: Coffin (1983:2) and Barnett (1979).

6. For more information on the role of the church in the persecution of gay and lesbian people see Grahn (1984), Martin (1984:342–43) and a bibliography compiled by C. Bidwell at the University of Alberta [http://www.ualberta.ca/~cbidwell/eses/eses-bib.htm].

7. For a discussion of Aboriginal rights, see Richardson (1989) and the Royal Commission on Aboriginal Peoples (1996).

8. The Mi'kmaw people spell the name of their nation "Mi'kmaq" as a noun and "Mi'kmaw" as an adjective. See comments by Bernie Francis, Mi'kmaw linguist, in the introduction to Knockwood (1992).

9. Thank you, Jackie Barkley.

10. This section was clarified during a conversation with Jeanne Fay. Thank you. Also see Muszynski (1991).

11. During the 1960s, when I began to develop an awareness of oppression, my first experience of being shocked by stereotypes was listening to comedy routines about Jewish mothers on Mike Nichols and Elaine May's recording, "An Evening with Mike Nichols and Elaine May" (Mercury Records, 1960). When I listened to Nichols and May's brilliant work again years later, I heard much more affection than oppression.

12. This quote can be found in any news source for September 11, 2001.

13. Andrea Dworkin connects racism and sexism in her analysis of the sexualization of Black and Jewish women in the United States and the sexual stereotypes of Poles and Roma (Gypsies) in pornography. See Dworkin (1981).

14. The literature on the witchhunts in Europe contain ample evidence of the linking of female sexuality with oppression. See Merchant (1980) and Starhawk (1982:183–219).

15. More information on the Indian residential schools can be found in note #13, Chapter Four.

16. I encountered several examples of this when I was working for CUSO in West Africa in 1985.

17. For more information on Black and First Nations children in white adoptive and foster homes see Johnson (1991), Ladner (1977), and Simon and Altstein (1992). There is an extensive bibliography of this subject on the Internet: "Reader's Guide to Adoption-Related Literature: Transracial Adoption" [http://members.aol.com/billgage/trnsracl.htm].

18. In Nova Scotia in 2001, foster parents receive $12.98 per day for a child under nine and $18.87 for a child over ten to cover food and shelter, and an annual clothing allowance of $471 for a child under four, $777 for a child between five and nine, and $1086 for a child over ten. On top of this there is coverage for medical expenses, emergencies, initial placement costs, school supplies, recreation, travel, special needs, extra-curricular activities, and special talent needs (Human Resources Development Canada [http://www.hrdc-drhc.gc.ca/socpol/cfs/foster_care/ns.shtml]). A parent on social assistance receives an average of $14.93 a day for everything (Government of Nova Scotia [http://www.gov.ns.ca/just/regulations/regs/esiaregs.htm]).

19. See McDougall (1991). In this article three graduates of the Shubenacadie Indian Residential School attack the school's critics. "'The Sisters of Charity deserved medals, instead of being criticized the way they were,' says Mrs. MacDonald. A lot of the negative stories are exaggerations or just plain lies, the three friends agree."

20. For an analysis of how women's interests are placed in opposition to their children's, especially at the fetal stage, by a society that does not value either women or children, see Mies and Shiva (1993:87–88).

Two Quotes: Breaking Silences, Healing

I do not wish my anger and pain and fear about cancer to fossilize into yet another silence, nor to rob me of whatever strength can lie at the core of this experience, openly acknowledged and examined. For other women of all ages, colors, and sexual identities who recognize that imposed silence about any area of our lives is a tool for separation and powerlessness, and for myself, I have tried to voice some of my feelings and thoughts about the travesty of prosthesis, the pain of amputation, the function of cancer in a profit economy, my confrontation with mortality, the strength of women loving, and the power and rewards of self-conscious living.
—Audre Lorde, *The Cancer Journals* (1980:9–10)

Hello from all the years of pain that I and my sons endured and all the pain of a bruised body and spirit. I want to make people aware of what can happen to them and their children and their dreams. Only then will life have a meaning and the pain go away and the nightmare end. It has been almost ten years and for me the healing is not complete. There is still a lot to do and a lot to be said and I expect to be around to do that. I can not rewrite my past or forget it. By speaking out I can also help myself and give my life a purpose and meaning and replace those old fears.

Fear and shame and failure are all the emotions that are experienced by a battered woman. I was born in a time when people did not reveal their personal problems. Emotions were kept inside, a secret. We all keep up appearances. And it is all part of early conditioning and very deep rooted. Battering and violence is not the taboo, speaking out against it is. It can only continue if we remain silent. I want to tell you to not be silent. Come forward. Be heard. The more that come forward the sooner we can change society's attitudes. Tell your story no matter how shocking. We must unite with one view. Do not cover up the bruises or your story.
—Jane Hurshman Corkum, "Presentation to the Dartmouth Task Force on Violence Against Women" (1991), as reproduced in the program for her memorial service, 2 March 1992.

Chapter Six

Step 3: Consciousness and Healing

In Chapter Four, I offered an analysis of the cycle that perpetuates oppression. It can be broken at many points. I think, however, that there is one point where the cycle must be broken in order for any other break to last. This point is the unconscious pain buried in each of us: the pain that causes us to use old survival strategies, without question, when a new situation looks anything like an old one; the pain we project on others and then punish them for it.

The oppression cycle makes it very difficult to organize the kind of social justice actions required to build a cooperative society. What makes justice possible is the amazing ability of human beings to grow in consciousness and heal. If unconscious pain is integral to the process of learning oppression, then consciousness and healing are necessary in the process of learning liberation.[1] Our means of liberating ourselves from oppression are organization and collective action, but without consciousness and healing our organizations will fall apart and our actions will tend to lead towards a repetition of the very oppression we are trying to change.

Unconscious pain is both individual and collective. For example, African-descended people, whether they have experienced individual abuse or not, carry the memory of slavery. Even when removed from the situation, peoples who have experienced oppression carry the scars. Jews, Roma, Palestinians, Armenians, Kurds, First Nations people, and many others cannot just walk away from the injuries of their histories. European-descended people as well, whether or not we have personal memories of childhood abuse, carry the larger cultural memories of the centuries when mistreatment of women, children, people of colour, and people who follow religions other than Christianity was made an acceptable part of Western society. I believe that all descendants of those who went through the Inquisition, from 1300 to 1700 CE, carry fears, distrust, and pain from that time, whether we are conscious of it or not. Starhawk calls the Inquisition "the abusive past of Western civilization."[2]

Consciousness raising and healing also operate at both individual and collective levels and come about through both individual and collective means. Consciousness in the individual can grow through such practices as journal writing, reflection, dream interpretation, reading, conversation, consciousness raising groups, meditation, therapy, counselling, silent retreat, ritual, research, observation, and analysis. Sometimes consciousness comes unbidden when something is pointed out by others or emerges into memory through flashbacks, a powerful experience, or finding out new information.

Collective consciousness comes through discussion, group study, collective action, and group reflection. The ideological tools of the powerful, discussed in Chapter Three, are usually working to dim our consciousness or give us false notions of the reality we live in; on the other hand, they also are important sources of information for our growth in consciousness.

In both individual and collective healing, speaking out is vital. It is the courageous act of breaking out of secrecy, privacy, and shame to contact others suffering similar pain that eventually leads to an understanding of the root causes. Speaking out becomes a collective movement, opening a role for writers, singers, artists, and historical researchers. For example, women, and now men as well, speaking out about their experiences of childhood abuse have led to a movement dedicated to eradicating abuse and healing its survivors. Likewise, some historians and archeologists have risked extreme academic discrediting and isolation to tell the stories I summarized in Chapter Two—stories of peaceful, woman-centred early societies, of the Enclosure Movement, and of the conquest of the Americas. By doing this, they provided the basis for a major transformation in the consciousness of white European and North American society. New consciousness offers an opportunity for healing.

As oppressive experiences—both individual and collective—are raised in one's consciousness, the pain that comes with them must be healed. On both the collective and individual level this requires emotional expression with trusted people in deliberate healing settings such as therapy or through informal gatherings, self-expression, or the arts. Healing can also come through organization and action. In both collective and individual healing, certain things taken away by oppression must be restored. These include participation in our future, the ability to make decisions, sexuality, anger, grief, friendship, trust, self-esteem, love of our bodies, love of the earth, a sense of connection to one another, the ability to link together around common concerns.

Healing can sometimes lead to a violent backlash against those who expose the issues. Breaking the silence can carry great risk. Jane Hurshman Corkum, quoted at the beginning of this chapter, was a determined fighter against woman and child abuse. She courageously broke silence again and again about her own experience as an abused woman. The quotation appeared in the program for her memorial service. She was found dead of a handgun wound on the Halifax waterfront. The police concluded that she committed suicide, but few of her close friends and colleagues believe that conclusion (Some Angry Women 1992:6–12). There were too many facts that contradict it, above all, the threats she received in the weeks leading up to her death. She was told to be silent or she would be silenced. Even if she did take her own life, it was a direct result of the years of abuse and the pressures put on her because of the outspoken public role she chose. She is one of many who have died, or suffered in other ways, for speaking out.

Backlash can also happen inside individuals and groups as the consciousness and healing progress. When a person is healing through counselling, for example, sometimes the process goes so far and then the old patterns of belief and behaviour cause the person to lash out violently and irrationally, as if the old patterns are cornered and fighting for survival. At the beginning of Chapter Four, I spoke of two experiences of groups that operated in a cooperative, consensus fashion for two years, then broke up suddenly, violently, and irrationally. Both groups were unusually powerful in their ability to create a setting in which people progressed quickly with their own healing. The sudden breakup may have been the phenomenon of "cornered patterns" on a collective level. It was truly as if "power-over" itself lashed back, terrified and fighting for survival. Perhaps this is what a "demon" is—the practices of "power-over," deeply rooted in people's scars. When there is an attempt to "exorcise" these patterns, from an individual or a group, the patterns fight back, almost as if they had a life of their own.

Every person has to find her or his own way to consciousness and healing. Sometimes it is important to work at it in a solitary fashion or with one other person; sometimes the process requires healing through activism or group dialogue. Both are necessary. Without individual healing, a person might destroy the groups she or he joins; without group healing, individual healing reinforces the private isolation that is the basis for "divide and conquer." Sometimes the process will seem to leap ahead; at other times there will be a plateau that seems to stretch on forever. Healing involves times of deep despair and pain; there are also times of joy and humour. The path always involves courage, honesty, self-examination, and listening, but it is different for everyone.

Those who work for justice must understand the differences in our healing paths. I get very angry when we waste our energy accusing each other of being "wrong" in our search for consciousness and healing. This sort of conflict is especially common between those who are currently in need of solitary or inner healing and those who are currently healing through collective action. The activists accuse the personal healers of "navel-gazing" while the personal healers accuse the activists of using action as a way of avoiding self-awareness.

I believe consciousness and healing make the difference between a person or group that gets some power and uses it against others who are less powerful and a person or group that gets power and works towards building a new society. Consciousness and healing melt the seals keeping the blueprint of oppression locked inside individuals.

Notes

1. When I use the term consciousness, I mean the concept of *conscientização* as developed by Paulo Freire, Amilcar Cabral, Ivan Illich and others. See Freire (1970) and Smith (1978).
2. Starhawk made this statement in a speech in Halifax, NS, on February 10, 1991.

Chapter Seven

Step 4: Becoming a Worker
in Your Own Liberation

The spiral of human liberation has been well documented.[1] It begins with breaking the silence, ending the shame, and sharing our concerns and feelings. Story-telling leads to analysis, where we figure out together what is happening to us and why, and who benefits. Analysis leads to strategy, when we decide what to do about it. Strategy leads to action, together, to change the injustices we suffer. Action leads to another round of reflection, analysis, strategy, action. This is the process of liberation.

Sandra Butler speaks of healing as a journey from victim, to survivor, to warrior (Butler 1978). Some dislike the word "warrior," but few have walked their own healing path without reaching a stage where further progress requires taking action to change the situation which caused the injury in the first place. This is the point where people become workers in their own liberation.

Reaching this transition does not mean that healing is complete, nor is it the end of private, individual healing; rather, a new stage is reached and a new need is felt. Healing requires taking action to save others from experiencing what you experienced. The task becomes more than recovery of yourself and your own life. It becomes necessary to find the power to change old and deeply rooted oppressions. Where is this power found?

There is a saying that comes from an old pagan tradition of Europe: "Where your fear lies, there lies your power also" (Starhawk 1987:9). Fear is often a guide to the areas in which the dominant society has particularly crushed and controlled you, and the reason you have been particularly crushed and controlled in these areas is because they are the sources of your power.

One of our sources of power as women is our ability to bear and nurture new human life. Men in power have made great efforts to take this power away from us by controlling our bodies and our reproductive ability. The "medicalization" of childbirth by mostly male doctors that began in seventeenth-century Europe has only started to be reversed in the last decade of the twentieth century. Childbirth and menstruation have been surrounded with fear and loathing, and the tradition—common in female-positive cultures[2]—of women being together at these times has been misinterpreted as men pushing women out of their company because they are "dirty."[3]

Sexuality is a source of power in itself, apart from its relationship to reproduction. Sexuality is a source of deep connection between people and wholeness within an individual; it triggers a release of emotion and creativity. Any society held together by hierarchical oppression must repress and limit sexuality, make it a fearful, filthy thing, link it with violence, and turn it into a sign of ownership rather than pleasure and joy. It is particularly effective to turn sexuality into a private shame, into something that divides people from one another, disguising our similarities, by making us hide our deep feelings from one another. In their film, *Not a Love Story,* Bonnie Sherr-Klein and Linda-Lee Tracy (1981) claim that part of the Nazi strategy was to flood conquered countries with pornography, thus using individual shame to separate people and reduce organized opposition.

Anger is a source of power. Anger should be an expression of our will directed against injustice. Anger, in this society, however, has been turned into violence without analysis, an excuse for more repression. We believe anger is something to be feared and controlled, in ourselves as well as in others. People in our culture, especially women, are afraid to be angry because they believe that no one will associate with them anymore, that they will be isolated and written off as "hysterical." Women are even told it will "spoil your looks."[4]

Sharing grief is a source of power that brings us very close to one another. Some other cultures that are closer to the earth, to themselves, and to each other, have wailers at funerals to ensure the expression of grief. Later, the wailers encourage story-telling about the deceased, laughter, and celebration of the memories.[5] In Western culture, grieving is not condoned. We stand in frozen politeness, talking as if we were attending an afternoon tea rather than a funeral, ashamed if we "break down." Children are told not to cry at a funeral because they might disrupt others' composure. Western funerals are a great boon to tranquilizer manufacturers.

Our bodies are a source of power. They carry us through our tasks and actions, give us pleasure and warnings, tell us directly the state of the earth we live on, and provide us with a wonderful thinking, feeling, moving, sensing instrument for carrying out our will in the world. Our experiences of oppression teach us to hate our bodies for their gender, their colour, and their connection to nature.[6] If we can love and appreciate our bodies, we can regain a source of power.

Friendship is also a source of power. Oppression maintains itself by putting us in competition with one another, making us distrust and distance ourselves from each other. Friendship is crushed by sexism and heterosexism, which try to convince us that closeness to another person can only be defined in sexual terms. Recovery of friendship gives us back the power of trust, equality, connection, value, and respect, and gives us the ability to become conscious, heal, organize, and act together.

A great source of power for all people is the process of linking our common problems and concerns. This requires breaking the bonds of shame and talking about our deep feelings. This is the process of confession, of "coming out," the beginning of consciousness raising. It is the source of the healing power of self-help groups, peer support, and counselling. Every time it happens, another movement for social change begins, because people are linked in struggle again, and we lose our shame. No wonder the churches would rather we confessed singly, privately, to a priest, or that we repeat a formula printed in a prayer book.

In developing the systems that keep us controlled and oppressed, those who have benefitted all along have zeroed in on the sources of people's power and concentrated their violence there. No wonder we feel fear whenever we approach one of these areas: our bodies, sexuality, friendships, grief, anger, shame. No wonder so many of us fear having any kind of power. No wonder fear can act as a guide to finding those areas of life where we have lost our history of collective power.

The next question is: What kind of power do we want? Many of the sources of power I list above are sources of "power-with," or authority. These are our key tools for building a new society, but are they enough, considering the extent of "power-over" we have to deal with?

When we are organized, we also have some means of gaining influence with those who have "power-over." These means include lobbying, advocacy, demonstrations, hunger strikes, and many, many more. But what about "power-over"? Do we want that? Can we make changes without it? Can we use it without becoming addicted to it as so many others seem to have become?

Followers of Gandhi would probably say no, we must use only the forms of power we want to see used in our new society.[7] I would like to be able to say that, but it seems to me that we must, at some points in our liberation, use "power-over." Sometimes there is little choice. Meeting young Nicaraguans who fought for their liberation convinced me of that. Their only other choice was to wait for death.[8]

In theory, cooperative people could use "power-over" for a certain specific purpose if they were conscious and had healed themselves to the point that they would not become addicted. The use of "power-over," like any addiction, hooks a person's unhealed, buried pain. I cannot imagine, however, that any of us are that conscious or healed. Perhaps all we can do is surround our use of "power-over" with as much consciousness and healing as possible, and devise checks and balances, held by a number of people, to be sure it is employed for the purpose originally intended and then discarded afterwards.

I say this because of the first experience I described in Chapter Four. I watched while a single person, using the tactics of "power-over," destroyed a workplace where "power-with," or consensus, had been working very well. As department coordinator, I had the means of "power-over" in that situation myself, given to me by the hierarchy of the larger organization within which we were working, but I was afraid to use it. I believed at that point that any use of power was wrong by definition. As a result, I watched a single source of hierarchical power destroy a well-established experiment in "power-with." I saw for myself how vulnerable a consensus process can be when even one person wants control. The department had been doing very good work and growing within the organization. I allowed it to become so weakened by the internal struggle that we could barely keep up with our daily tasks. Then, when the organization decided to close the department, blending our work into a larger unit, we could not organize ourselves to resist. I lost my job, and eventually the department's mandate was cut altogether.

Thinking back on the situation, I believe that I could have taken control of the department in a traditional, hierarchical manner until the situation was dealt with, then returned it to its consensus-based method of operating. There would have been problems, of course, caused by this course of action, but the department would not have been in a weakened internal state when it was hit by an external attack. It could have continued doing useful work. It would have been important to be open with everyone about what I was doing and why. I learned from this experience not to fear my own share of "power-over" nor to consider its use wrong in all circumstances.

I also struggle with the power I have over children. I try to use consensus as much as possible with the children in my life, but sometimes it is necessary for an adult to control the situation for the health and safety of all concerned. I do try to communicate what I am doing and why, but all the same, I do use my power over children.

While weighing these choices, it is very important to remember that "power-over" breeds "power-over," no matter what we do to prevent it. Its use must be a last resort. For real change, we must develop new and creative ways to use "power-with" and "power-within."

As a community development worker, I found the challenge was always how to support the empowerment of individuals and groups in such a way that they will value and practise "power-with" rather than grab "power-over." Because "power-with" is not generally understood or supported in our culture, oppressed people sometimes form organizations and learn skills only to turn and dominate someone less powerful. Sometimes when individuals learn to speak up and stop disempowering themselves, they begin to dominate their group, using nepotism and manipulative tactics to maintain their power. "Power-over" is the only model they see.

The image I have for the work of empowering oppressed people is one of trying to walk on a muddy ridge between two plough furrows. You pull yourself up on the higher soil, only to slide over into the next low spot. Another image would be one of those little games, encased in plastic, where the object is to put a ball bearing into a depression in the cardboard base. Too little speed and the bearing falls short; too much and it scoots over. The challenge is to support the empowerment of people, but with healing and consciousness as part of the process, so that the power they learn is used in a cooperative fashion. It is also important to remember that the community development worker is not in charge; the people involved are. We can encourage new leaders, provide information, and teach skills, but in the end, the use of the power gained is decided by the recipients. The surrounding society, which values competition and contains the wounds people have experienced in the past, is still the environment in which we function at this point.

This, then is the process of liberation—moving from consciousness and healing, individual and collective, to the analysis and strategy-building required to change society. As I explained in Chapter Four, I believe we must experience oppression in order to learn how to participate in oppressing others. I also believe that the opposite is true; we must be engaged in working towards our own liberation in order to become allies to others in their process of liberation. I explain my view of this connection further in the next chapter.

Notes

1. See note #3, Chapter One.

2. When a female-positive society comes into contact with colonialism, women are gradually forced to become subservient to men. Descriptions of the process can be found in Villamarin (1975) and Schlenker (1975). Because there are no known societies that have escaped colonialism, there may be no truly gender-equal cultures left. However, many retain aspects of their former female-positive nature, including matrilineality, female positive polygyny, women's right to be together in retreat during menstruation, clan mothers (North America) or queen mothers (West Africa), women's law-making councils, high female to male sex ratios, or a positive attitude toward homosexuality. Examples of these societies are (or were, some are now extinct):
   - Cherokee, Iroquois, Keres Pueblo, Narragansett, Pocasset, Sakonnet (North America), (see Allen 1986);
   - Chibcha (Columbia), (see Villamarin 1975);
   - Choctaw (U.S.), (see Schlenker 1975);
   - Hopi (U.S.), (see Schlegal 1984);
   - Huxian Region (China), (see Kristeva 1977);
   - Innu, Wyandot, Iroquois, Cherokee (Canada, U.S.), (see Leacock 1977);
   - !Kung (Southern Africa), (see Draper 1975);
   - Lemba (Zaire), (see Schoepf 1987);
   - Mojave, Navajo (U.S.), (see Midnight Sun 1988);
   - Poncas (U.S.), (see Ware 1960:28);
   - Trobriand (Papua New Guinea), (see Malinowski 1927:25–32);
   - War Khasis (Bangladesh), (see Das Gupta 1989:78–81).

   For further reading on remnants of female-positive cultures, see Cavin (1985:99–137).

3. A colleague, Jean Arnold of New Brunswick, spent several years living with the Shoshone people in Wyoming, U.S. She talked about how hard women worked and how much they, and she, looked forward to the quiet, restful time they would spend in the "women's lodge" during their menstruation. Unfortunately, in many post-colonial societies, this practice has been interpreted as negative. Women are banned because they are "unclean" or dangerous at this time. For a discussion about how women begin to be seen as dangerous to men during a transition from a female-positive to a patriarchal society, see Starhawk (1987:50).

4. For excellent commentary on the socialization of women's anger, see Lerner (1985).

5. My first introduction to the tradition of wailers was a conversation in 1978 between a Cree elder, Stan Cuthand of Saskatchewan, and a visiting Maori judge from New Zealand's Maori courts. They compared many aspects of their culture, and one was their way of mourning. This was an exciting

discovery for me, raised as I was in a tradition that represses grief. For a written description of wailers and other grieving traditions in various cultures, see Counts and Counts (1991).

6. Katherine Gelday has made a dramatic film about how women's body image is eroded in patriarchy, *The Famine Within* (Gelday 1990), (see also Orbach 1978).

7. See Raghavan (1973).

8. This information comes from personal conversations with young Sandinista soldiers in Nicaragua in March 1980. During the long war that led to the revolution in July 1979, children served as look-outs, message-runners, bomb-makers, and graffiti-writers for the anti-Somoza forces. They also threw bombs under tanks, since they were too small to be seen by the tank's drivers. As a result of this activity, Somoza's troops were ordered to shoot children on sight. This put many young people in a position where their choice was to wait and die or join the Sandinista forces, (see also Guillén 1979). For a general background history of the Nicaraguan Revolution, see Kinzer (1991).

A Journal Entry: Racism and Sexism

Gay Pride Week, 1990

This morning I attended a workshop on racism. I went to listen to the leader's experiences and to struggle with his reality from a position defined by my basic assumptions about being an ally: that is, he knows, I don't; I'm here to listen and understand and become an ally through contributing my effort and resources to the struggle in ways he defines and controls.

Then, this afternoon, he fought against a group of lesbians struggling to have some woman-only time in our gay and lesbian club. We tried to explain that we, as women, are excluded by the way men behave, express and display their sexuality, and use space. In the presence of darkness and liquor, they awaken frightening memories for many of us. We don't want prime time at the club, just some time to be among our own and not have to be squeezed into the leftover corners and feel afraid, again.

I know the issue for him is exclusion because of his (and many others') history of being turned away from, beaten up in, or asked to leave white bars.[1] I understand that it looks like any other exclusion to him, but it's not. We are not white bar owners who don't want Black people in our establishments. We are women trying to struggle against the omnipresent domination of men. He couldn't hear us. Ready to accept our willingness to be allies in the struggle against racism, he was not ready to be an ally in the struggle against sexism.

I can't then say, "I won't be your ally anymore," like a child on a schoolyard. We're talking about peoples and history, what my people have done to his, and his gender has done to mine, over hundreds of years. It's not him or me as individuals. I must be an ally in the struggle against racism simply because I see it. If he cannot see our relationship as also man to woman, there isn't much I can do. My hope that all of us can engage with each other to end oppression fades a little.

Note
1. There is a long history in Halifax of African-Nova Scotian people being harassed in and excluded from bars. This problem led to violent disruption on the streets of the city during July 1991. The leader of this workshop was a leader for years in the efforts of African-Nova Scotians to have equal access to bars.

The Globe and Mail, Tuesday, March 19, 1991

FEEDBACK / *'Women's issues' in this country have traditionally been framed in terms of white, middle-class experience —*

the time has come time to tackle the concerns of the rest: native women, black women, Asian women, immigrant women . . .

Moving toward a new emancipation

BY CARMENCITA R. HERNANDEZ
and JANE WALSH

Women's Day Doesn't Have Much To Do With Women, said the headline on a recent Globe and Mail article in which writer Donna Laframboise complained that the event focused on racist issues instead of such topics as child care and contraception.

The origins of International Women's Day can be traced to protests by women textile workers over a fire in New York City in the first decade of this century that killed 146 women workers. The women protested against the overcrowded, dangerous working conditions and exploitative wages they encountered in that city.

In 1910, at the Second International Conference of Socialist Women, Clara Zetkin proposed that March 8 be set aside each year in commemoration of women's struggles. The first International Women's Day was therefore celebrated in many countries on March 8, 1911, with the theme of "international female suffrage" — a victory that our sisters in South Africa still cannot celebrate.

In Toronto, the International Women's Day Committee was formed in the spring of 1978 as an anti-capitalist, anti-patriarchal organization. Through years of debate and struggle, it evolved to reflect the realities faced by women in Toronto.

The theme for Toronto's 1987 Women's Day was "fighting racism and sexism together." Carol Allen and Judy Persad gave a speech that moved and touched everyone: "Last year . . . we said we are going to build a new women's movement in Toronto — a women's movement which will integrate the fight against racism and the fight against sexism. Racism and sexism have to be integrated into the movement because they are already in our lives. The women's movement must represent all women — the fight against racism is everybody's fight."

Racism is a priority for the women's movement in Canada today. It is appalling that Ms. Laframboise calls a day devoted to racism "an opportunity for solidarity lost and squandered." It is frightening that she holds a degree in women's studies. Under the banner of feminism, Ms. Laframboise sets out maintain that celebrations in Toronto are "not relevant to most women."

Ms. Laframboise points out that it is not the first time that racism has been given a high profile. As early as 1977, the National Action Committee on the Status of Women recommended that the federal Human Rights Commission conduct an inquiry into the socio-economic and discrimination problems of immigrant and visible-minority women. Since the 1980s, immigrant and visible-minority women's organizations have put forward their issues.

Self-determination is key for the liberation of all women. Because we understand how male dominance has controlled women's lives, we can also make the links to racism and imperialism in women's oppression.

"Stop the racist war from Oka to the Gulf — make the links," which was the 1991 theme of Toronto's International Women's Day, should be of interest to all women in this country. Canada spent millions on war in the Persian Gulf while social programs at home are at risk.

It is disheartening that there is still a perception among white and liberal women that the movement "belongs" to them — a claim to the ownership of a feminism built on a white, Western model. This leads to white women resisting, or giving little credence to, issues that are critical to the lives of native women, black women, Asian women and immigrant women.

Such concerns, which include racism, immigration, refugees, language training and employment equity, may not appear to be women's issues to some.

Women of colour have been at the forefront in demanding that these issues be addressed by pushing and challenging the assumptions and the politics of the women's movement. Articles like Ms. Laframboise's make changing the framework of the women's movement in Canada truly painful.

Traditionally, "women's issues" have been framed in terms of white, middle-class experience. Addressing them has not resulted in advances for all women. Feminists must look at who has set the agenda. The advancement of women is not a linear struggle. The issues of oppressed women in this country need attention.

At a national conference called Moving Forward: Creating a Feminist Agenda for the 1990s, held at Trent University last June, keynote speaker Rozena Maart said, "If feminists cannot move forward toward the emancipation of all women, we should not hesitate to call it anything else but self-aggrandizement."

Clearly some women have made the links.

———

Carmencita R. Hernandez is chairwoman of the Coalition of Visible Minority Women. Jane Walsh is Southern Ontario representative for the National Action Committee on the Status of Women.

Chapter Eight

Step 5: Becoming an Ally

In the early 1990s, I co-led a workshop called "Unlearning Racism" with a friend and colleague who is African-Nova Scotian.[1] When you begin to teach something, you find out what you do not know. This workshop was truly a learning adventure for me.

Leading anti-racist education is akin to tip-toeing through a mine field. Sometimes we could feel the group carefully skirting a possible blow-up; sometimes we stepped on a mine. When this happened, there was an explosion, an angry backlash from some of the white participants. We conducted the workshop five times before we made it all the way through without the process being completely derailed by conflict.

Following one of our most explosive workshops, I began to list the different reactions of the white participants to this process of unlearning racism. Later, the descriptions began to fit into three rough groups: 1) the "backlashers," who deny the existence of racism while making racist statements and expressing outrage that they are forced to listen to stories of racism; 2) the "guilty," who personalize the issue and become defensive and paralyzed; and 3) the "learners" or "allies," who use any opportunity to learn more and then act on what they learn.

"Backlashers" are those who say: "That all happened a long time ago; don't blame me," or "I'm a good person; I've never done anything nasty to anyone of a colour different from mine; don't blame me." Any excuse will do for a "backlasher" who is trying to avoid responsibility for racism—"It's a theoretical problem," "I feel silenced by Black people; I can't say anything right," "My brother worked in Jamaica and said there it's the other way around," "Don't jump on me, I was just asking a question," "Some of my best friends are Black," and above all, "I'm not racist." There are always deeply felt emotions coming through these statements, primarily anger. These participants fail to see the collective aspect of the oppression, cannot see their own privilege, and take too little personal responsibility.

The "guilty," on the other hand, fail to see the collective aspect of the oppression and take on too much personal responsibility. They are crushed, unable to move. They feel powerless and sometimes react angrily against the person or situation they think disempowered them by making them aware of the problem. They often seek forgiveness from someone they see as a representative of the oppressed group. Privilege is often invisible to the "guilty" group, too, or if they see it, it adds to their immobilizing guilt.

"Backlashers" rarely understand the meaning of oppression for those who experience it; the "guilty" are all too aware of it, but they are inclined to react to their own oppression and that of others as if nothing can be done. "Backlashers" tend to think the current North American model of "democracy" is working and people could solve their problems if they tried. The "guilty" also believe there is democracy here, and that they, as voters and citizens, have the power. If something is not working, it must be their fault.

Members of the "ally" group, on the other hand, are much more critical of the real power structures of North America and the world. They look at the world from a "structural" perspective. They have an understanding of themselves as part of a people or various peoples. They understand that if something is done to another member of their own group, it could have happened to them. For example, they understand that, if a woman is raped, it is not because she asked for it, or dressed seductively, or went where she should not have; it is because she is a woman, and it could happen to any woman. Likewise, "allies" understand that, as part of various oppressor groups (white, male, able-bodied, heterosexual, middle or above in the class structure), they did not individually bring the situation about and they cannot just reach out with goodwill and solve it. They understand that they must act with others to contribute to change. They believe that to do nothing is to reinforce the *status quo*; not to decide is to decide; if you are not part of the solution, you are part of the problem. Many "allies" still drive themselves too hard and try to do too much, but they do understand that they are part of something much larger and older than they are. They take responsibility for helping to solve problems of historical injustice without taking on individual guilt. Most look for what they can do, with others, in a strategic way, and try to accept their limitations beyond that.

This latter understanding of power relationships is rare in our society. The political/economic/ideological system that keeps power in a few hands has been very successful in developing methods of childrearing and education that ensure North Americans do not understand power and how it works.[2] Those who do understand have usually worked their way to their insights through their own experience, reflection, and efforts to work towards social change.

"Allies" are distinguished by several characteristics:

- their sense of connection with other people, all other people;
- their grasp of the concept of social structures and collective responsibility;
- their lack of an individualistic stance and ego, although they have a strong sense of self;
- their sense of process and change;
- their understanding of their own process of learning; their realistic sense of their own power;
- their grasp of "power-with" as an alternative to "power-over;"
- their honesty, openness, and lack of shame about their own limitations;
- their knowledge and sense of history;
- their acceptance of struggle;
- their understanding that good intentions do not matter if there is no action against oppression;
- their knowledge of their own roots.

These are the characteristics of allies; they are also characteristics that mark people who are well advanced in their own liberation process.

Because of the connection I see between the experience of powerlessness and the need to find safety through controlling others, I believe that an experience of oppression is necessary for a person to learn to be an oppressor. Margaret Green's account of her anti-racism therapy groups strongly supports this connection. She tells a story about a woman working on her difficulty welcoming new immigrants who came to the advice centre where she worked:

> I suggested she try welcoming me. As a Jew and a foreigner I could never have enough of it, I explained, and besides, no one had ever welcomed me to England anyway. She tried. She was extremely timid and tentative. I asked if she had ever been made to feel welcome. She burst into tears; no, of course she hadn't. There was no warmth for her in her family; she had always felt unwanted. (1987:194)

After this and several other examples, Green concludes: "One of my assumptions is that no one would ever willingly choose to take on the role of oppressor if they themselves had not been systematically oppressed" (195).

Because of my observation that people who approach other oppressed people as allies are those who are involved in their own process of liberation from oppression, I also believe that one must be in the process of liberation from one's own oppression to become an ally in another's liberation. Green's experience again supports mine. She says:

> You cannot be proud of other cultures and delight in their richness if you are not proud of your own. By "proud" I don't mean the defensiveness which hides feelings of shame and inferiority and I don't mean that one doesn't question certain aspects of one's culture. A sense of one's own rich roots is however essential if one is to meet on an equal level with a person from a different background. (1987:196)

I don't mean to suggest that everyone who experiences oppression becomes an oppressor, and everyone engaged in their own liberation becomes an ally. Far from it. What I am saying is that I don't believe it is possible to become an oppressor without experiencing oppression nor become an ally without being involved in your own experience of liberation.

Learning About Yourself as an Oppressor

The process of learning about one's own oppression is different from learning about one's self as an oppressor. The former process has experience clearly as a base. It is a transition from experience to consciousness through reflection.

When learning to see yourself as an oppressor, the experience is by definition hidden from you, because part of the process of becoming a member of an oppressor group is to be cut off from the ability to identify with the experience of the oppressed. It is this lack of empathy, this denial that anyone is hurt (at least, anyone viewed as fully human) that makes oppression possible. When the oppression is not part of your own experience, you can only understand it through hearing others' experience, along with a process of analysis and drawing parallels.

Many people resist beginning the process of becoming an ally because it is so difficult and painful. Is it more difficult and painful than your own liberation? I think so. I have found it much harder to understand and accept myself in my oppressor roles than in those where I am the oppressed.

The righteous anger of understanding one's own oppression releases a great deal of energy and propels the process forward. Facing fear often releases energy and produces a major shot first of euphoria, then of good, solid self-confidence. The process of bonding with others dealing with the same oppression creates a deep level of sympathy and understanding, a growing pride in one's recovered identity, and a shared language that is as satisfyingly secret as the "pig latin" of childhood.[3] There can be lightning fast communication among women in a room or among lesbians in a room. There is laughter or a flurry of glances, a smile, a comment with a double meaning, and you know "you" all understood, and "they" did not.

Coming to understand one's identities as an oppressor is often an enervating process. It means being shut out from someone else's secret language; it involves accepting your inheritance of a shameful and evil past. There is guilt, that useless and draining non-emotion. There is always that unsettling knowledge that you cannot see what is going on as clearly as the oppressed group can. The oppressed always know a great deal more about the oppressor than the oppressor knows about the oppressed.

Understanding one's own position as an oppressor, without being completely immobilized, also requires a balance between understanding oneself as an individual and as part of a collective reality. This balance is rare in the culture we live in. Modern Western thinking is extremely individualistic. Our ties to the land and our own history, community, and culture have been severed. With so little understanding of ourselves as part of a collective entity, it becomes very difficult to figure out our own responsibility for patterns larger than ourselves.

Failure to understand collective structures leads to what Kate Kirkham calls "overpersonalization." In her article "Teaching About Diversity: Navigating the Emotional Undercurrents," she says:

> Many majority group members do not move quickly or comfortably back and forth between their individual identity and their identity as a member of a racial or gender group in this society. If they do think of themselves as a member of a group, it is often associated with negative emotions: feeling stereotyped or threatened, etc. Therefore, majority group members may enter a discussion less prepared to sort out what is being said about the behavior of numbers of whites (or men) as experienced by others and the impact of their own individual behavior.... When asked to re-

spond to the question of who really is racist and/or sexist, many majority group individuals in my research and teaching experience, assume: "If I didn't intend something as racist or sexist then it is not racist/sexist." In other words, the general criteria they use in testing for racism/sexism is an overpersonalized one. They believe that personal motive determines the presence of racism or sexism in interactions. (Kirkham 1988/89:51)

"How To"— Becoming an Ally

Having written that title, I must now admit that I cannot tell anyone exactly how to become an ally. I can, however, use my growing analysis of the process and my experience to offer some guidelines. Most people in our society do not yet see the connections between different forms of oppression or even have a general sense of how oppression works. Therefore, we still find ourselves dealing in most instances with one form of oppression at a time, and in a given setting, we are either in the role of oppressed or ally. I hope these observations will be as useful to you as they have been to me when I find myself in the ally role.

1. It is important to be a worker in your own liberation struggle, whatever it is. Learn, reflect on, and understand the patterns and effects of oppression, take action with others, take risks, walk towards your fear to find your power.

2. Try to help members of your own group understand oppression and make the links among different forms of oppression.

3. I cannot overstress the need to listen. Listen and reflect.

4. Remember that everyone in the oppressor group is part of the oppression. It is ridiculous to claim you are not sexist if you are a man or not racist if you are white and so on. No matter how much work you have done on that area of yourself, there is more to be done. All members of this society grow up surrounded by oppressive attitudes; we are marinated in it. It runs in our veins; it is as invisible to us as the air we breathe. I do not believe anyone raised in Western society can ever claim to have finished ridding themselves completely of their oppressive attitudes. It is an ongoing task, like keeping the dishes clean. In fact, the minute I hear someone claim to be free of the attitudes and

actions of a certain oppression (as in "I'm not racist") I know they have barely begun the process. Humility is the mark of someone who has gone a ways down the road and has caught a glimpse of just how long the road is.

There is a parallel here with the principles of the twelve-step addiction recovery process. Just as the twelve-step programs teach that the process of healing from addiction is never finished, so it is with the process of unlearning oppression. A white person never becomes non-racist but is always a "recovering racist," more often referred to as "anti-racist."

There is another reason members of an oppressor group are always oppressors, no matter how much individual learning we have done: until we change the politics and economics of oppression, we are still "living off the avails."[4] We would not be where we are, doing what we are doing, with the skills and access we have, if we did not have the colour, gender, sexual orientation, appearance, age, class, or physical abilities we have. Resources and power continue to come to us because we are members of the dominant group in relation to the particular form of oppression where we seek to be allies.[5] So, until we succeed in making a more humane world, yes, we are racist (or ageist, or classist, or heterosexist, and so forth). Understanding this is part of learning to think structurally rather than individually. It is part of avoiding overpersonalization of the issues.[6]

5. Having accepted that every member of an oppressor group is an oppressor, try not to feel that this makes you a "bad" person. Self-esteem does not have to mean distancing yourself from the oppressor role; it can come instead from taking a proud part in the struggle to end oppression. This involves learning to separate guilt from responsibility. Guilt means taking on all the weight of history as an individual; responsibility means accepting your share of the challenge of changing the situation. Members of oppressor groups spend a great deal of energy in denying responsibility for oppression. What would happen if all that energy could be put to work figuring out how to end it?

6. Remember that in the oppressor role you cannot see the oppression as clearly as the oppressed group can. When people point out your oppressive attitudes or language to you, your first response should be to believe it. Ask questions and learn more about the oppression going on in that particular situation. Try not to leap to your own defence in

one of the many ways oppressors use to deny responsibility for oppression. Self-defence is an overpersonalized response.

It is true that you will likely meet members of the oppressed group who will want to claim that every little thing is oppressive and use it as a focus for their anger. You will also perhaps find members of the oppressed group who will try to use your efforts to unlearn oppression to manipulate you. It is all part of the process—their process. The point is not to defend yourself; it will not work anyway. If you can deal with your own defensive feelings, you can turn the situation into a discussion that you, and perhaps everyone else, can use to learn more about the oppression, and you will be less vulnerable to manipulation. The defensiveness, or guilt, is the hook for the manipulation.

Also, if you can use your own experience of liberation to understand the anger of the oppressed, you will be able to accept it as a member of an oppressor group, not as an individual. Leave their process—working through their anger—to the oppressed group. Give your attention to your own process—becoming an ally. Then we can all participate in the process we share, ending the oppression.

7.   Count your privileges; keep a list. Help others see them. Break the invisibility of privilege.[7]

8.   If you hear an oppressive comment or see an example of oppression at work, try to speak up first. Do not wait for a member of the oppressed group to point it out. Sometimes this draws a response of "Oh, I don't mind," "It was just a joke," or even anger directed at you from a member of the oppressed group. That person may be speaking out of their internalized oppression, or you may be off base. Just accept it, if you can; admit it is not your experience. More often you will find members of the oppressed group grateful that they did not have to raise the issue for a change.

9.   You must be patient and leave lots of room for the greater experience of members of the oppressed group, but there are also limits. If it becomes clear over time that you are being used or mistreated, say something and/or leave the situation. Here is an example: a group is interested in having you present as an ally for reasons of their safety or your contacts, legitimacy, or resources but is not ready to offer you any information or support. The message might be: "Just shut up and do everything we tell you and don't ask questions." It is also hardly fair for

the members of the oppressed group to direct all their anger, over a long period of time, at a well-meaning would-be ally. This is not reasonable treatment for anyone. It is fair for you to ask them to decide: do they want you to leave, or will they provide you with some support in your efforts to become an ally?

10. Try to avoid the trap of "knowing what is good for them." Do not take leadership. They are the only ones who can figure out what is good for them, and developing their own leadership strengthens their organizations. It is fine to add thoughts or resources to the process by asking questions of the individuals with whom you have already built up some trust and equality, who will not take it as coming from an authority greater than themselves just because you are a member of the oppressor group. It is not all right to take time at their meeting or public gathering to present your own agenda or to suggest in any way that they do not understand or see the big picture.

11. Never take public attention or credit for an oppressed group's process of liberation. Refuse to act as a spokesperson, even when reporters gravitate to you because they are more comfortable with you or curious about you. You should speak in public only if members of the oppressed group have asked you to speak from your point of view as an ally or to take a public role on their behalf because speaking out will be too dangerous for them.

12. Do not expect every member of the oppressed group to agree; does your group agree on everything?

13. Learn everything you can about the oppression—read, ask questions, listen. Your ignorance is part of the oppression. Find people in the oppressed group who like to teach and who see value in cultivating allies in general or you in particular. Ask them your questions. Do not expect every member of the oppressed group to be ready and willing to teach you. When you are in the ally role, you have privileges and comfort in your life that members of the oppressed group do not have because of the oppression; they may not want to also give you their time and energy so that you can learn about them. They may not have the time or the energy.

14. Support the process of unlearning oppression with other members of your own group. Do not usurp the role of communicating the experience of the oppression; that one belongs only to members of the oppressed group. You can, however, share with other members of the oppressor group the journey of becoming an ally; you can help break through others' ignorance of the oppression. Members of your own group might hear you when they cannot hear a member of the oppressed group.

15. Remember that you will probably have to go out of your way to maintain your friendships and connections with members of the oppressed group. Our society is set up to separate different groups. Without a little extra effort, you will live in different parts of town and never cross paths. On the other hand, do not fall over backwards. It is not good to ignore the friends and support base you have already established because you are spending all your time working at the barriers or becoming a "hanger on" of the oppressed community in an inappropriate way.

16. Try not to look to the oppressed group for emotional support. They will likely be ambivalent about you, happy on one hand to have your support, annoyed on the other at your remaining oppressor arrogance, your privilege, the attention you get as a member of the dominant group. Their energy is needed for their own struggle. This does not mean you will not receive support from members of the oppressed group, sometimes more than is warranted. For example, look at the praise men get for doing housework when women still do the vast majority of it. Try not to expect the oppressed group to be grateful to you.

17. Be yourself. Do not try to claim the roots and sense of connection that a history of oppression can give to a community if it is not your own. Do not become what the Mi'kmaw community calls a "Wannabe." Dig into your own roots. The oppressive history of the group you belong to is a burden you carry. Search out the history of allies from your group as well. Dig even deeper than that. Every group started out as a people with roots in the earth somewhere. Find your own connection with your people's history and the earth. If it is absolutely untraceable, find appropriate ones and rebuild roots and connection in the present for yourself. But do not try to steal someone else's; you cannot anyway.

18. Be yourself. Be honest. Express your feelings. Do not defend your internalized oppressor attitudes; say that it hurts to discover another piece of it. Do not sit on your doubts (except in public gatherings or meetings where you are an observer); ask them of someone you trust. The key word is ask. Assume that you are a learner; good learners are open.

Margaret Green provides a brief summary of the process of becoming an ally in matters of race:

> There is usually a dawning realization that being an ally to a person of colour involves knowing a great deal about one's own background, remembering with pride one's own history of resisting injustice as well as one's participation in the history of racism. It involves being able to listen and tolerate the differences between people, expecting to make mistakes, knowing that people of colour will be angry with you to the point of what appears to be unreasonableness, and learning to take it. It involves also knowing that people who view you as an oppressor may try to mistreat you—but this you need never accept. (1987:204)

"How To"— Working with Allies when you are a Member of the Oppressed Group

When the shoe is on the other foot; that is, when you find yourself in a situation where it is your oppression under consideration, the same principles are in operation, but they are applied a little differently. Here are some guidelines, from my experience, for the situations where you are a member of an oppressed group dealing with allies.

1. Make a clear decision about if, why, when, and how you will work with allies. Do you want to work with allies at all? What can allies offer you that you would find useful? It is easy to know what you do not want members of the oppressor group to do; figure out what you do want them to do. Are there certain times, places, meetings, tasks, and functions where allies would be useful and others where their presence would be inappropriate? Be clear and conscious about your degree of openness to allies. Make sure everyone agrees on what is appropriate or at least can live with the decision without undermining the functions of the people who come in as allies. Working with

allies brings a certain kind of struggle; be sure you are ready to enter into it.

2. Allies need support and information. Decide before you begin working with them what you can offer. There needs to be someone in your group who has the patience for teaching allies more about the oppression you are dealing with.

3. Be wise and canny about who is really an ally. If you end up with members of the oppressor group who are acting out of guilt, trying to replace lost roots, taking centre stage, or telling you what to do, you will end up with more frustration than help. Also, beware of people who have no consciousness of their status as a member of the oppressor group or who are unaware of their own oppression in other areas.

4. Do not lump members of the oppressor group together, thinking of them as all "white" or "straight" or "male." Remember that everyone is or was also a member of an oppressed group and that people identify more with the parts of themselves that have been oppressed. You may see a woman as white, when she thinks of herself as Jewish; or you may think of a man as male, when he identifies himself primarily as gay.

5. You must listen too.

6. Be kind. Allies are taking a risk, exposing themselves to a situation that is bound to be painful at times.

7. Try to be clear about who is the enemy. There are lots of people who hate you and want to oppress you, punish you, and keep you in your place. There are the rich and powerful who are creating, sometimes deliberately, more of the oppression you suffer daily. Allies are usually well-meaning people without a great deal of power in the system. They are more vulnerable to your anger because they lack power and because of their very desire to be an ally. Do not waste resources fighting with them.

8. Be yourself; be honest; express your opinions; be open. Working with allies is all part of a learning process for you too.

Working for Liberation and Becoming an Ally:
Using the Lessons Back and Forth

A person who is involved both in struggling for liberation as an oppressed person and in becoming an ally to other oppressed groups has a wonderful opportunity to learn by constantly drawing parallels back and forth. For example, when I want to figure out what I should do in a situation where I am the only white person, I begin by asking myself what I would want a man to do if he were the only one in this situation with a group of women. I do not necessarily do what I would want that hypothetical man to do, but thinking about it provides some guidelines.

Likewise, my own experience as an ally has given me a great deal of insight into the value of allies to the groups where I work on my own liberation. I observe the groups I belong to interacting creatively with allies or mistreating allies, and I can use my own experience as an ally to understand what is going on and figure out what to do about it. My own experience as an ally has also taught me how oppressed groups often overlook the information and insights allies can give them, especially when it comes to building a strategy for action.

Balance and Clarity

For each guideline I have written in this chapter, I can think of a time when the advice would be misleading. I know sometimes the guidelines almost sound contradictory. That is because the essence of the path to becoming an ally is balance and clarity. One must balance patience and confrontation, flexibility and limits, boundaries and allowances, learning and opinion, humility and self-confidence, your own oppression and others' struggles. Clarity comes from observation, reflection, and analysis in a specific situation. In the light of this process, the complexities of the relationships between the oppressed and allies can resolve into beautiful, clear patterns. There is even sometimes a feeling of being "crystal clear" inside. It is a "knowing." Then you know what to do and what will happen when you do it.

Notes

1. Our workshop was based on exercises adapted from CUSO (1990), Katz (1978), and Obedkoff (1989). It was published by OXFAM-Deveric in Halifax, NS (now available for two dollars from "Unlearning Racism," c/o Fernwood Publishing, Box 9409, Stn. A, Halifax, N.S. B3K 5S3), (see Bishop and Carvery 1994).

2. See Miller (1981, 1983, 1986).
3. "Pig latin," the way we spoke it as children, involves moving the first letter to the end of every word. "Struggle against oppression" becomes "truggles gainsta ppressiono."
4. "Living off the avails" is the charge brought against pimps who live on the earnings of prostitutes they control.
5. See McIntosh (1990) and Jensen (1998, 1999).
6. Dartmouth, Nova Scotia, playwright Wendy Lill (now also Member of Parliament for Dartmouth) has explored how systemic racism emerges through individuals despite a positive attitude, pleasant personality, and kind motives. See her powerful plays *The Occupation of Heather Rose* (1987) and *Sisters* (1991).
7. See note #5.

A Journal Entry:
How Not to be an Ally: An open letter to the young man who spoke at our memorial rally on December 6th

On the evening of December 6, 1990, several hundred people gathered in Halifax's Grand Parade Square to remember the fourteen women killed at L'Ecole Polytechnique in Montréal a year earlier. Their murderer had yelled at them that he hated feminists. Over the days leading up to the anniversary, the radio had reported men taking over microphones at similar memorial rallies to shout abuse at the women present, even to threaten them with a fate similar to the Montréal women. Some women stayed home from the December 6 rally out of fear; those who came were watchful and tense. The invited speakers were all women. During the rally, a young man took the microphone, obviously uninvited. Later I wrote this entry in my journal:

Dear young man:
I know you meant well when you took the microphone, uninvited, and spoke to us at the December 6 rally in memory of the women who died in Montréal a year ago. Your "contribution" added the only sour note in an amazingly powerful and expressive series of events that evening. You provided a crystal clear example of how not to be an ally to an oppressed group.

Your first error was your disrespect for the women who organized the rally. If you wanted to speak, why didn't you find the organizers and arrange with them in advance? That would have given the group the opportunity to think about it together and make a decision about when and how you might, or might not, fit in. Instead, you put one woman, the one holding the microphone, on the spot, forcing her to make a complex decision instantly and alone. You also spoiled the careful ordering of the speakers, which had been working beautifully.

Your second mistake was your complete insensitivity to the meaning of the event and the deep emotions and painful experiences that underlie it. Women have been subject to male violence and abuse for five thousand years. We all carry a deep fear of it somewhere inside us. The events we were recalling that night bring the fear very close to the surface. Also, the news all week had carried stories of men taking over the microphones at similar events and yelling abusive insults at the women present. When you took the microphone, in a manner that made it obvious to all present that your speech was unplanned by the organizers of the event, I'm sure almost all the women present tensed up completely, as I did. I immediately started calculating the distance between us, as I was standing on the steps near you and could have tackled you and grabbed the microphone if your intent was abusive. Massive fears welled up inside me with thoughts of who else might be there. Were there other men present considering violence? If you roused them, or if I took action to stop you, would they react with their voices, hands, even weapons, against the women present? Is there a copycat in the house? I discovered later that I was not the only woman nearby who was going through exactly the same series of thoughts.

Finally, why did you have to speak at all? You went on far too long and said very little. Do you not think we know what we need? Do you not know we need to see our own kind at the centre of attention at an event that is about our oppression? Do you not respect our need to speak and listen among ourselves, to channel our emotions and share our thinking, in reaction to an event that touched us deeply? Can you not stand back and listen respectfully for even a brief time; can't you accept that you cannot share our experience? I cannot imagine going to the front and taking the microphone at an event where Black people are working through something of importance to their liberation—or people with disabilities, or immigrants, or francophones, or Jews, or First Nations people. To be present as an ally is a privilege, and the role of an ally is to listen and learn and trust that the people who are central to the event know what they need. When they trust you and know you well enough, they will ask you to do something specific to support their efforts.

You made all of these errors before you even opened your mouth. Then there was what you said. No, we will not take what Marc Lepine did with "a grain of salt." We can't. And yes, some men are our allies, but not when they take centre stage at our event to spill out their misplaced defensiveness.

Perhaps you really do want to be an ally. I'm glad, but you have some learning to do. First, you must sort out your own business—your pain at facing yourself as a member of an oppressor group, your confusion between individual and collective responsibility, your inability to distinguish between support and patronizing and, above all, your need to set aside your ego and LISTEN.

I hope to see you around again, quietly listening at the edge of the crowd.

Chapter Nine

Notes on Educating Allies

Much of my work for the past thirty years has been in the field of adult education, specifically popular education. The aim of popular education is to overcome the internalized oppression that marginalized people carry around in our thinking and help us move toward liberation. Popular education includes reflection and action. It is often illustrated as a spiral that moves from experience to reflection, then to analysis, strategy, action, and begins again with the experience gained from taking action.[1]

As I began to think about my own role as oppressor as well as my experience of being oppressed, I joined many other educators in experimenting with education designed to "unlearn" the oppressor roles we have all learned. I think of it as educating allies.[2]

Principles
The key principle of educating allies is its *structural* and *historical* approach. In Canada, much of the education we do about the differences among people is based on a *liberal*[3] approach. The education is aimed at individuals, with the purpose of helping us understand our differences and learn more about each other's experience and cultures. The assumption is that if we increase the knowledge and change the attitudes and behaviours of individuals, then the organizations, institutions, and society as a whole will also change. It also assumes that people are basically equal.

Educating allies, on the other hand, is based firmly in the structural and historical principles of popular education, wherein people are seen as part of larger systems, shaped by our context. The assumption is that we can change our institutions and culture only through collective organization and action. We are seen as products of history, rooted in a class system that makes us very unequal in our access to power, legitimacy, and resources. The purpose of educating allies, as with all popular education, is to equip ordinary people to make change by acting together.

Spiral Model of Learning*

Reflection * feelings
* reactions
* hopes
* fears
* challenges
* surprises
* contradictions

Analysis * history
* power structure
* dynamics
* patterns
* trends
* context
* leverage points
* actors
* interests
* allies/enemies

Placing Ourselves
* class   * values
* race   * assumptions
* sex   * ideology
* age   * learning style
* language
* sexual orientation
* religion
* ability/disability
* national origin

Action
* do it!
* becomes the next
  experience for
  reflection

Strategy
* implications
* goals/objectives
* planning for action

* Also called the Action-Reflection Model or the Conscientization Model
Adapted from: The "Core Model" of Learning, Centre for Christian Studies,
Toronto, Ontario
CUSO Education Department, *Basics and Tools: A Collection of Popular Education
Resources and Activities* (Ottawa: CUSO, 1988)
Arnold, Burke, James, Martin, Thomas, *Educating for a Change* (Toronto: Between the Lines, 1991)

That said, often those who would like to educate allies are working
within structures that do not allow this kind of educational goal to be
pursued directly. Many are limited to introducing the concept of becoming an ally in a liberal setting—a classroom, organization, or workplace.
However, if the person introducing the concept is an ally, working on the
liberation of her/himself and others, the activities specifically labelled
"education" will be only a small piece of a more sustained and collective
strategy to end historical inequalities in the larger institution.

The position of an ally seeking to educate others in an institutional
context can be very complicated if there are other types of "diversity
education" taking place in the organization. If the "diversity education" is

being done badly, it will leave at least a sour taste in everyone's mouth and at worst a backlash against learning anything about equality issues. Even if it is done well, I have mixed feelings about diversity education. On one hand, the basic purpose of diversity education is to make institutions function better. Often these are institutions that in the end contribute to oppression. An example is "the business case for diversity." Diversity educators talk about how "diversity training" cannot be successful if the company does not understand the connection between diversity and the bottom line.[4] As explained in Chapter Three, I see the structure and purpose of corporations, their values and methods of functioning, as one of the basic causes of oppression. Diversity education designed to improve the functioning of such organizations is for me a contradiction in terms.

On the other hand, well done diversity education can teach people the concepts, attitudes, and skills necessary to develop teamwork among people from different groups. This knowledge and the skills that go with it become part of the individuals who participate. They can be transferred to other settings—families, communities, voluntary organizations, future workplaces. I must leave the contradiction inherent in diversity education for my readers to ponder. Every situation is different, and every ally in a liberal institution has to decide what course to follow.

Returning to the primary principle of educating allies: it is an understanding of oppression as structural and historical. Within that larger framework, there are some specific assumptions for educating allies. These are: 1) we all have the experience of both being oppressed and oppressing others; 2) our experience of oppressing others is often hard to access because privilege is invisible; and 3) our oppression of others is based on unhealed, and often unconscious, pain from our own experience of being oppressed.

Nothing is Sometimes Better

Before going on to discuss how these principles unfold in practice, I want to stop and give a warning: ally education must be done well, by a teacher skilled and experienced in this type of education. Otherwise, it is better not to do it at all. In ally education, the aphorism that "any little bit helps" is not true.

If you try to introduce the concept of allies with what one of my teachers called "hit and run" education,[5] it tends to act like a vaccine. A single class or workshop can encourage people to pick up a useful term or two that helps them pass as open-minded and tolerant without them really having grasped the concepts involved. This can lead members of oppressed groups to trust them when they shouldn't. Also the individuals or organization can check "diversity" off of their list—"been there, done that"—without understanding the continuous, structural, and collective nature of unlearning oppression. Ally education must be part of an ongoing effort—either a course long enough to work through the concepts for several months or a long-term commitment to change in an organization.

Above all, if a person attempts ally education who does not thoroughly grasp the concepts or demonstrate being an ally in their own actions, or does not have the skills to deal with the deep emotions that will be stirred up, oppressive attitudes can be solidified and confirmed, or backlash triggered. Those who suffer the most from this backfiring of good intentions are those who are most vulnerable in the situation because they are targets of oppression in the first place.

Please, if you are not sure of the concepts involved in this type of teaching or if you do not have the skills to deal with strong emotional reactions, do not attempt to lead ally education. Seek out more of it yourself instead.

Reflecting on Experience

The heart of educating allies, as in all popular education, is reflection on experience. As explained in Chapter Eight, even though we are taught not to recognize our experience of being oppressed, it is there to be observed, because oppression can be seen, heard, and felt by those who are its targets. On the other hand, it is difficult to be aware of one's experience of oppressing others. For one thing, part of the oppression is that we are cut off from our ability to empathize with the oppressed. If we are aware of it at all, we tend to get defensive or write it off as not very serious—"They are just whining." For another thing, the privileges that we obtain from oppressing others are invisible to us. For a third thing, oppression is structural. We derive benefits from being male or white or straight or able-bodied without taking any personal action against a woman, a person of colour, a gay/lesbian/bisexual person, or a person with a disability.

When educating allies, it is necessary to connect participants with their experience of being oppressed in such a way that they can draw parallels to their position in society as oppressors. I have experimented with three methods of doing this. Two involve reflection on experience outside of the session. One of these is the "Flower of Power" exercise; the other is the "Oppression/Privilege Workshop." The third, a simulated reversal, brings the experience right into the session.

The Flower of Power

The "Flower of Power" was invented by Enid Lee[6] and further developed by members of the Doris Marshall Institute in Toronto (Arnold et al. 1991:87). It involves a three-layered flower drawn on a piece of paper. Each participant receives a copy. In the centre of the flower, various forms of oppression, such as sex, race, ethnicity, and age, are listed. The inner petals are blank. Participants fill in their own social identity in relation to each form of oppression listed in the centre—are they male or female; white or a person of colour; have they suffered from ethnic oppression, such as the oppression of the Irish by the English or the Ndebele by the Shona?[7] In the original exercise, the outer petals are also blank; working together, participants fill in the group they think are dominant in our society in regard to each oppression. If the time for the exercise is short or if you suspect the group will spend all their time arguing about which group is dominant and miss the point of the exercise, the outer petals can be filled in before the flower is photocopied for the participants.

After the inner and outer petals are filled in, it is helpful to have participants colour in the sections where their inner and outer petals match with one translucent marker or highlighter, the pairs where they do not match with another. This makes the participants' experiences of oppression and privilege in different parts of their identities stand out vividly.

An alternative to the "Flower of Power" is the "Power Line," an exercise I learned from Eileen Paul of Resourcewomen.[8] It serves the same function as the "Flower of Power," but the dominant group is already defined in some cases and does not need to be in others. Participants are asked to imagine a line drawn down the middle of the floor. One side has power and privilege, the other side is oppressed. As different forms of oppression are called out, people go to one side of the line or the other. For example, when the issue is sex, men go to the privileged side of the line, women to the oppressed side. When we are considering ethnicity, those who have experienced oppression by another ethnic group go to one side, and those who have experienced being in a dominant ethnic group go to the other. There are sometimes people in the middle who have experienced both or neither side of a given form of oppression.

When sexual orientation comes up, I do not ask people to go to one

The Flower of Power

side of the line or the other, but instead explain the risks gay and lesbian people face when we become visible. I do this early on so that any gay or lesbian people present do not have to worry about what they will do in this situation. A few gay and lesbian people have expressed anger that they did not have the chance to go to the oppressed side of the line and talk about their oppression, but most are grateful to remain invisible.

The "Flower of Power" works best when group members are intellectually oriented and all have literacy skills. The "Power Line" is more active, brings more laughter and energy into the workshop, and avoids the question of who in the group cannot read and write the dominant language. The "Flower of Power" provides more room for learning about which groups are dominant in our society; the "Power Line" gives less room for this discussion and is useful when you think a group is likely to spend all of its time debating who is dominant, diverting attention from the primary lesson of the exercise: that is, that we have all been on both sides of the line. As mentioned above, the discussion of which group is dominant can also be avoided with the "Flower of Power" if the inside spaces are already filled out before the flower is copied for the participants.

Both exercises give a good starting point from which participants can reflect on their experiences on both sides of the line and the lessons learned on each side that can be useful when one is on the other side. The group can focus their discussion around the questions: "What did you learn from filling out the "Flower of Power"/participating in the "Power Line?" "What are your experiences in the areas where you are a member of the oppressed group?" "What are your experiences when you are a member of the dominant group?" and "What have you learned from your experiences of oppression that could be useful to you when you are the oppressor trying to become an ally?"

In my experience, these exercises are unfailing indicators of how ready the group members are to learn to be allies. When people argue at length about which group is dominant, become angry about sorting themselves into oppressor and oppressed, and reject the basic premises of oppression inherent in these exercises, the rest of the workshop will involve dealing with anger, denial, and resistance to the process of learning to be allies. When people understand and accept the basic concepts of oppression inherent in these exercises and move on quickly to using them for reflection, you know the rest of the workshop will be spent moving ahead on the road to becoming allies. These early reactions make perfect sense as indicators of the class or workshop to come, of course. Ally education is based on the same assumptions about oppression contained in the two exercises. Participants who reject the underlying premise in the exercise will have trouble accepting the remainder of the class or workshop.

The "Oppression/Privilege Workshop"
The "Oppression/Privilege Workshop" provides another means of reflecting on participants' experiences of being a member of both oppressed and oppressor groups. At the beginning of the exercise, people are asked to form small groups of two to four members, who experience the same form of oppression. This can be done in an open "marketplace" style, where one person might call out "Who would like to work with me on language oppression?" and another person, or several others join her/him. When the groups are formed, each one gathers around a sheet of flipchart paper to answer the question: "I know I am in the presence of _____ (the form of

oppression chosen) when …" For example, "I know I am in the presence of body image oppression when someone makes a nasty comment about my dress size." The group should label their page with a heading at the top and fill in as many indicators of that form of oppression as they can fit on the page.

When the groups have filled their pages, put them up on the wall with enough room between them to fit another set of flipcharts. Ask each group to share what they have written. If there is time, allow them to expand upon their points and answer clarifying questions from the rest of the group.

After all the groups have spoken, ask the participants to form new groups, also with two to four people in them, based on shared membership in a dominant group. Again the "marketplace" method can be used. This time, ask the groups to complete the sentence: "What privileges do we get from being _____?" For example, "What privileges do we get from being white?"

When they have filled their pages, have them put them on the wall between the pages that are already there. If there is a pair, put them together; for example, if you have a page for oppression based on disability and one for the privileges of being able-bodied, put them side-by-side. Again, ask each group to present their page, expanding and answering clarifying questions if there is time.

When all the pages have been presented, put up three flipchart pages labelled "Oppression" "Privilege" and "Both." Ask the group to identify patterns that they see in the sheets on the wall. For example, a pattern under the heading "Oppression" might be "Stigmatization, assumed to be bad and inferior." A pattern under the heading "Both" might be "Rigid boundaries, no shades of grey." Under the heading "Privilege," the participants in a 1996 workshop saw one pattern as: "See yourself more (in the media, etc.) but recognize yourself less!" Take time to discuss them. When there are as many patterns identified as you have time for, ask the question: "What can we learn from our experiences of oppression that helps us become allies when we are in the dominant group?"

Simulated Reversals

Simulated reversals are exercises that put the participants from a dominant group briefly in the position of those who suffer the oppression you are studying. Sometimes just listening to members of the oppressed group tell stories about their experience can be a reversal in itself, since it is unusual for members of the oppressor group to listen to the stories of the oppressed. Participants sometimes react with anger and a feeling of being "silenced," "made powerless," and "forced to listen." These responses provide an excellent opportunity to help participants understand that these experiences and feelings are common for members of the oppressed group. Listening to stories can also bring out feelings of guilt. It is important to reflect on this response, making clear the distinction between feeling guilty (bad, wrong, an evil person) and taking responsibility for a structural inequality that is not your fault but gives you unfair privileges.

Other reversals take place in structured simulation exercises. An excellent example is the "Blue Eyes, Brown Eyes" simulation for understanding racism. The exercise was originally developed for a grade-three class by Iowa teacher Jane Elliot in response to Martin Luther King's assassination in 1968.[9] The Association of Black Social Workers of Nova Scotia uses this exercise well in their racism workshops. When participants arrive, they are divided according to eye colour. Brown-eyed people are taken into the meeting room and given a briefing on the next exercise, a quiz on Black history in Nova Scotia. People with lighter eye colours stay in the hallway, and are told to stand back against the walls and refrain from talking to each other. Conversation draws an immediate rebuke from the supervisor of the hallway.

When the blue-eyed people are allowed into the meeting room, they sit around the edges of the room, behind the brown-eyed people. The Black history quiz begins. The brown-eyed people, already briefed, have the answers and are praised and admired for giving them. A blue-eyed student is occasionally recognized. If the answer is correct, she or he is told: "That's pretty good for someone with blue eyes." If the answer is not correct, the hapless person is belittled and told: "What can you expect from blue-eyes?" The effect is very rapid. When I went through the exercise it took me about ten minutes to completely lose my self-confidence and begin making wrong answers even when I knew the correct ones.

When the issue is poverty, an excellent reversal simulation is the board game and workshop "The Poverty Game" (Monkman et al. 1983). It was developed by a group of low income single mothers in Dawson Creek, B.C. They based the roles in the game on their own lives.

Another way to bring about a reversal is through a well done guided fantasy. There is an excellent example in Cooper Thompson's *A Guide to Leading Introductory Workshops on Homophobia* (1990). This imaginary journey leads participants into a world where same-sex relationships are the norm. Heterosexuals must hide and lie to preserve their jobs, apartments, loved ones, and personal safety. Fantasies can put people deeply into an imaginary experience. They should be led only by a facilitator experienced with the method.

Any kind of reversal simulation requires plenty of time for reflection afterwards.

A Note on Willing and Unwilling Participants

The best educating allies sessions are, of course, those with people who have chosen to take part. If participants have come primarily because of guilt, it can be difficult to get things moving, but if they have actively chosen to struggle with their oppressive attitudes, for whatever reason, they are for the most part a great pleasure to work with. It is important with a group like this to share your plans, negotiate the agenda before you begin, negotiate the process as you go along, make yourself vulnerable and express your struggle with your oppressor habits, and concentrate the energy of the session on building strategy.

When participants are present because someone else—their boss, their constituents, their union human rights committee—has forced them to be there, the situation is completely different. This group will actively resist your leadership, block and disrupt the process, argue with you whenever possible, and sometimes even write oppressive graffiti on your files, flipcharts, handouts, even the walls. If they succeed in reducing the leaders to defensive arguing, their oppressive attitudes will be reinforced. In a group like this, it is not helpful to share your plans, negotiate process, or make yourself vulnerable, and concentration on building strategy is a waste of time.

The "Flower of Power"/"Powerline" exercise and the "Oppression/ Privilege Workshop" assume voluntary cooperation. Unwilling participants can easily sabotage them. A resistant group, in my opinion, needs a strong experience of reversal. Put them through at least a powerful series of testimonials or, better yet, an exercise like "Blue Eyes, Brown Eyes" in which they experience oppression. They will react with anger. Help them process their response. Your main goal is to help them see that the injustice they have briefly tasted is the full-time experience of the oppressed group.

A Note on Emotional Responses

As explained in Chapter Four, at the core of our roles both as oppressor and oppressed is the unhealed hurt of our own experiences of oppression. As a result, any educational activity designed to unlock these experiences, no matter how academic, will also arouse strong feelings. For those who experience the oppression under discussion, the frustration comes from the defensive, angry or guilty reaction of those who don't. It can be yet another experience of oppression. For those who are in the dominant group in relation to the oppression under discussion, there is frustration because of their difficulty in seeing the oppression, as explained in Chapter Eight.

In "Teaching About Diversity: Navigating the Emotional Undercurrents," Kate Kirkham of Brigham Young University talks about this source of emotional response on the part of dominant group members when race or gender are discussed in a university classroom:

> Individual majority group members do not hear or see in their day-to-day interactions the very examples the minority person offers as proof of the existence of racism or sexism. Certainly majority group members do not pass on stories to each other about what they did to contribute to sexism in their organization. The research on sexual harassment, for example, has recorded that it is a few of the men who do most of the harassing. The problem is that the behaviors of many of the men may not make it obvious who is the one who will later harass. Several men may "enjoy" a sexist joke but only one may continue his "enjoyment" of sexism by harassing women he works with in the organization. However, the men that allow the joke, all "look" like potential harassers. The men may individually (i.e., personally) dismiss or tolerate the joking without seeing how it fuels the one or two men who will continue to bring inappropriate sexual conduct into the workplace. The women who hear or hear about the joking may be weary of all those who allowed it. The men who allow joking, language or inappropriate discussion of women's appearance to occur at one point in time will not be present later when the behavior of other men becomes even more severely sexist. (1988/89:53)

Kirkham's example illustrates the frustration of a discussion on gender or race for members of the dominant group, particularly if they understand human relationships to be personal only and fail to see the structural elements. Another of her examples, also mentioned previously, shows this gap in understanding even more clearly:

> When asked to respond to the question who really is racist and/or

sexist, many majority group individuals, in my research and teaching experience, assume: "If I didn't intend something as racist or sexist then it is not racist/sexist." In other words, the general criteria they use in testing for racism/sexism is an overpersonalized one. They believe that personal motive determines the presence of racism or sexism in interactions.

An example of this assumption is present in the pattern of reactions of a majority group member in a graduate organizational behavior course during a discussion of racism and sexism in the workplace. Every comment made by a woman or minority student in the class was responded to by him (as soon as he had a chance) as if they had been directing their comments to him personally therefore indicting his intentions. He resented this and kept saying so with increasing emotional intensity. With some assistance, he identified the core reason for his reactions. He became aware that he was using what he thought was intended as the only legitimate criteria. If the point someone was making did not fit what he thought was intended in an example, then it was not an example of racism or sexism. Because he was emotionally defending what he thought were personal and unfair accusations, he could not broaden his understanding of racism and sexism. Once he realized that others were using criteria that included intended and unintended outcomes of behavior, he could better understand their examples.

An additional insight came from the above class discussion and indicates the usefulness of surfacing underlying assumptions that trigger emotions in a discussion. Many of the majority group members, who had been quick to label a minority group member as over-sensitive, became more aware of how their own version of over-sensitivity was showing up with just as much emotional conviction behind it. (1988/89:51)

I once asked a colleague how he became an ally to women. He said: "I finally understood that I may not be a perpetrator of violence against women, but I'm a perpetuator." Many others have not yet taken this step from understanding oppression in personal terms to understanding it as a structural reality. The result is that they cannot hear the structural reality discussed without feeling accused of something terrible and reacting with either guilt or anger.

When the setting is one in which deep feelings are expected, the framework and skills will most likely be in place to deal with emotional responses when they emerge. For example, in Margaret Green's work with women exploring their racism, the setting was a therapy group and Green herself is a therapist (Green 1987). This is an ideal situation, with concepts and tools specifically designed for exploring emotion, for exploring the painful memories that underlie oppressive behaviour.

In other settings, the emotions connected with the topic may not be as easily integrated into the discussion. As Kate Kirkham illustrates in her article quoted above, she uses classroom discussion to explore the underlying assumptions students have about the legitimacy of the subject, their definitions of racism and sexism, their concept of what constitutes "proof" that racism and sexism exist, and their methods for defining what is a problem and how big or small a problem it is. As she says in her article: "Ferreting out the core assumptions … enables the emotional intensity to be more richly explored for all involved in a discussion" (1988/89:49).

Whatever tools you have for processing the emotion in your educational setting, you will be called upon to use them when you enter the arena of educating allies. If you are not confident of your skills in handling emotional response, get some training before trying any experiments. As explained above, you can easily do more harm than good by venturing into ally education without the proper tools.

Analysis

After reflecting on the experience of oppression, it is important to move on to exercises designed to help the group understand what oppressive structures are and how and why they are put in place and maintained. There are many tools you can use for this: drawing diagrams, making human sculptures, acting out skits, putting yourself in the position of someone responsible for creating an oppressive society (as in the example used in Chapter Two). There are good instructions for how to use these learning tools in other books, so I will not repeat them here.[10]

I will, however, mention one simple analysis exercise that has worked well in my experience. Write out a series of questions on a flipchart or in a handout, such as:

> What do people in a dominant group gain from oppression? (or white people from racism, men from sexism, straight people from heterosexism, depending on the topic of the workshop)
> What do people in a dominant group lose from oppression?

What responsibility do people in a dominant group have to end the oppression?

What power do people in the dominant group have to end the oppression?

What do people in the dominant group need from those who suffer from the oppression in order to help end it?

Participants work on the questions in small groups and report back.

In my experience, there is a temptation to skip over analytical work, perhaps because it is a critical, intellectual process, and we live in a society where many people have been put down and shut out by those who use only this method of teaching—and make it into a competitive activity—in our schools and universities. Do not skip over it. Analysis in small groups can be very revealing and exciting and provides an essential basis for the steps that follow.

Skills

Another important aspect of educating allies is building participants' skills for identifying and responding to oppression. Possible activities include examining our everyday language, identifying the keys to recognizing oppression, developing role-plays of typical situations in different settings, and working with clippings or photographs to develop awareness of oppression.

The racism workshop I developed with Valery Carvery (Bishop and Carvery 1994) includes an exercise from Judith Katz (1978:115–16). Small groups list all the words or phrases they can think of with "light," "fair," or "white" in them; then all they can think of with "dark" or "black" in them. Next they mark which of these have a negative and which a positive connotation. They share their lists and reflect on them. This exercise invariably makes people take a new look at language they have always taken for granted.

For identifying oppression at work in various settings, we include an exercise from the Doris Marshall Institute called "When I see, hear, feel" (Arnold et al. 1991:89–90 and CUSO 1990). In small groups, participants complete the sentences: "When I see ... when I hear ... when I feel ... I know that racism is at work."

Working with photographs and clippings can be fun and revealing. It is depressingly easy to collect a portfolio of examples of any form of oppression. You can then make several copies and have participants analyze them in small groups and report back. The challenge is to see how many examples they can find in the documents they have been given.

Action

No course, workshop, or conference aimed at educating allies is complete without a plan for action. It helps if you give people a handout with the steps involved in planning a strategy (see page 142), ask them to work through all or part of it, and have them bring it back to the rest of the group. At least look at what changes people want to make, who has the power to make those changes, who should be involved, and what leverage points[11] are available to the participant, or participants, to move the process forward. Work on these pieces of the strategy in the workshop to be sure participants understand the principles involved in analyzing an organization that they want to change, even though the ultimate power is not held in their hands.

If people take part in the workshop as individuals, they must work out their action plans as individuals, but they can share them and make contracts to call one another at some point in the future to ask how each other's plans are coming along. When people participate in groups or are all part of one organization, the process of building a strategy for action is a more complex and satisfying one. The plan can be very specific and can include determining different roles for different people and setting meetings in the future to evaluate progress and adjust the plan.

Reflection, Evaluation, Closure

When the time available for a workshop or course is very full, as educating allies sessions always seem to be, it is tempting not to save enough time to close properly. This is a mistake. The closing process ties together the loose ends, gives a sense of completion and helps participants be conscious of their learning and take the experience away in a useful form.

Reflection is a time for participants to go back over the session and talk about what they have learned, on paper or aloud.

Evaluation means collecting feedback from the participants, aloud or in writing, that will help improve the session the next time it is offered.

Closure should be quick and energetic, something to get people on their feet, say a final word, and feel a clear ending to the process. There are many tools for this. For example, ask people to sum up their feelings about the workshop in one sentence, and then have each say their sentence in rap-rhythm, to the accompaniment of everyone clapping their hands and snapping their fingers. Another method uses a ball of wool. One person sums up her or his feelings about the workshop and throws the ball of wool to someone else, holding on to the end of the wool. The next person says how they feel and throws the ball, again hanging on to the piece of wool. At the end you have a web of wool woven back and forth, connecting everyone in the group. Comment on the connections among you, and lay the web carefully on the floor. Because there are so many useful sources in print, I will not describe any more methods here.[12]

A Note on Homogeneous and Mixed Groups

It makes sense that members of an oppressor group should work together to overcome our problem. We should avoid taking any energy away from the group we oppress by making them listen to our ignorance or asking them to teach us. Some have used such settings very effectively, particularly because being away from those we oppress allows for completely open exploration of attitudes without fear of hurting someone. Margaret Green in her method of working with women to unlearn racism demonstrates such work at its best (1987).

The pitfall of all-oppressor groups, however, is that they can easily slip into being too comfortable. Good education treads an important line between being too comfortable and too threatening. The facilitator of an all-oppressor group must be careful to create an educational design that presents challenges to the participants.

When I first decided to deal with my own racism and contribute to the struggle against racism by developing a workshop, I began by talking with several Black colleagues and friends about the idea. All but one opposed the idea of a white facilitator leading an all-white workshop on racism. They felt that the misconceptions white people hold about Black people and our tendency to deny racism would go unchallenged. It is hard for us to see our own racism, no matter how long we have been working at the process of unlearning it.

Because of these tendencies to develop blind spots and too much comfort in oppressor-only groups, mixed groups do work well for educating allies. However, it is very, very important that the members of the oppressed group present understand the purpose and process of the workshop and agree to take part. If possible, they should be paid or honoured in some way as resource people.

Another way of dealing with the inequalities between oppressor and oppressed in a workshop is to design two parallel processes that interact.

Members of the oppressed group work on the questions from their point of view; for example, "What are the stages you have gone through in coming to understand your oppression?" Members of the oppressor group work on the questions from their point of view; for example, "What are the stages you have gone through in your process of becoming an ally?" Later both groups report and reflect together.

A third method is to design a session intended to look at several forms of oppression and how they interact. Small groups or individuals reflect on their oppression, all using the same questions. Later they make presentations and all reflect together on the relationships among oppressions. The "Oppression/Privilege Workshop" described above is an example of such a process.

When a workshop is reflecting upon an invisible form of oppression, there is no way at the outset to tell who is or is not a member of the oppressed group. In this case, always assume you are working with a mixed group and make sure your language is inclusive. It also works well to make a rule at the outset that members of the oppressor group must hide their identity. In a heterosexism workshop, straight people learn a great deal from having to hide their wedding rings, change pronouns when talking about their partners and refrain from saying, "of course, I'm heterosexual, but. ..." It is very important to reflect on this experience later in the workshop.

Homogenous or Mixed Leadership Teams?

The questions that come into play when deciding about homogenous or mixed groups of participants all play a part in decisions about the leadership as well. There is a spectrum of opinion, from those who believe the leadership should be made up only of those who experience the form of oppression in question, through those who prefer mixed teams, to those who believe that the oppressor group should be working on their own problem separately. There are advantages and disadvantages to all of these options.

Leadership by the oppressed group in question can be limited by lack of understanding of the processes the potential allies must go through. Also, there is always the question of whether the energy required could perhaps be better used in the struggles of the leaders' own people, rather than in educating allies. It is easy as well to put participants in a position of "damned if they do, damned if they don't." For example, when I participate in heterosexism workshops, I want participants to express their op-

Building a Social Change Strategy

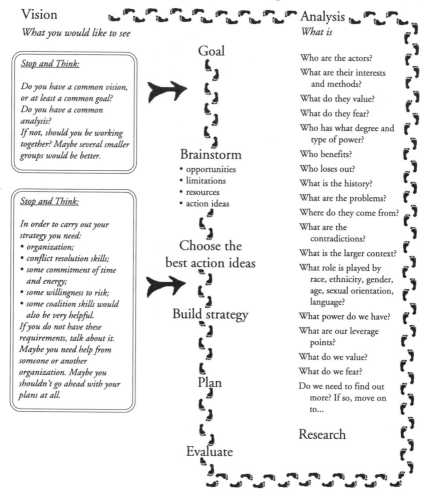

Theory of Social Change

Vision
What you would like to see

Analysis
What is

Goal

Brainstorm
- opportunities
- limitations
- resources
- action ideas

Choose the best action ideas

Build strategy

Plan

Evaluate

Research

Stop and Think:

Do you have a common vision, or at least a common goal? Do you have a common analysis? If not, should you be working together? Maybe several smaller groups would be better.

Stop and Think:

In order to carry out your strategy you need:
- *organization;*
- *conflict resolution skills;*
- *some commitment of time and energy;*
- *some willingness to risk;*
- *some coalition skills would also be very helpful.*

If you do not have these requirements, talk about it. Maybe you need help from someone or another organization. Maybe you shouldn't go ahead with your plans at all.

Who are the actors?

What are their interests and methods?

What do they value?

What do they fear?

Who has what degree and type of power?

Who benefits?

Who loses out?

What is the history?

What are the problems?

Where do they come from?

What are the contradictions?

What is the larger context?

What role is played by race, ethnicity, gender, age, sexual orientation, language?

What power do we have?

What are our leverage points?

What do we value?

What do we fear?

Do we need to find out more? If so, move on to...

pressive attitudes so that I can work with them in the learning process, but sometimes I do not want the pain involved in hearing those sick old clichés again!

On the other hand, leaders from the oppressed group have direct experience of the oppression to communicate, and the experience in a workshop of reversing the usual roles of oppressor and oppressed can raise responses which provide rich opportunities for reflection.

Leadership by and for an oppressor group has the same problems as a homogenous group of participants—the facilitators can reinforce misconceptions and the process can become too comfortable. However, it is very important for members of the oppressor group to take responsibility for the oppression and to push one another to make changes without asking the oppressed group to spend energy on them once again.

Mixed leadership has the benefits of both—the communication of experience and challenge of having members of the oppressed group in leadership; and the comfort and knowledge of becoming an ally that members of the oppressor group can provide. One potential drawback is that the leadership team can become so involved in their own struggle to maintain a good working relationship across divisive histories that attention to the participants' needs can suffer.

Reflections on Educating Allies

I have done many different kinds of adult education in the past thirty years. No two sessions are ever alike, but I have found nothing as unpredictable as educating allies. Even if the sequence of exercises is exactly the same, the workshops are totally different experiences. Difficult emotions are involved: hostility, guilt, denial, fear, embarrassment, pain. The experiences being communicated are powerful. Both of these things can also be said for sessions where people are working on their own form of oppression, but for some reason the mix in a group of allies is more complicated and explosive. As I have experimented with ally education, the process has gradually become more predictable to me, although there are still many surprises. I expect this learning to continue far into the future.

Educating allies is also a very satisfying form of education. Bridges are built on the spot, goodwill and risk-taking are obvious, communication takes place across the barriers of centuries, and experiments are initiated which have immediate importance in the process of building a new, more cooperative society. According to my analysis, this is exactly what we must do if we can hope for a future on this planet. Any degree of new learning or successful experimentation that unfolds during these sessions gives me great hope.

Notes

1. The basic principles of popular education can be found in the work of Paulo Freire (1970, 1972, 1973). There are many resources on popular education. My favourites are Arnold and Burke (1983), Arnold, Barndt and Burke (1986), Arnold et al. (1991), CUSO Education Department (1985/88), and Kuyek (1990).
2. There are many resources for educating allies in particular forms of oppres-

sion. A good starting point on unlearning racism and heterosexism are the materials listed in Chapter One, notes #4, #5 and #6.

3. See the explanation of liberalism in the glossary.

4. See Velasquez (1998).

5. Thank you to Hélène Moussa for this term. She used it many years ago and I have used it ever since.

6. Enid Lee is author of *Letters to Marcia: Anti-racist Education in School* (1985).

7. The Ndebele and Shona are two antagonistic ethnic groups in Zimbabwe. I have found it is a good idea to give two examples of ethnic conflict, one between two white peoples, the other between two Black peoples. This helps participants understand the difference between ethnicity and race. Perhaps the Hutus and Tutsis of Rwanda would be familiar to more people at this point because news coverage of the 1994 civil war in Rwanda brought their conflict to the attention of North Americans. See National Film Board of Canada/Alter-Cine (1996).

8. Resourcewomen provided training and skilled consultants for low-income women's organizations in the United States. It was part of the Center for Community Change in Washington, DC.

9. A film, entitled *The Eye of the Storm,* recording the original "Blue Eyes, Brown Eyes" experiment, was made in 1968. A more recent video, *Blue Eyed* (Elliot 1995), includes footage of a group of adults participating in the exercise and an interview with Jane Elliot. There is also a book on the exercise, including interviews with the original grade-three students twenty years later, (see Peters 1987). Another powerful video of a classroom experiment in learning about race and class, useful in the education of allies, is *War Between the Classes* (1985), from Marlin Motion Pictures, 211 Watline Ave., Mississauga, ON, L4Z 1P3.

10. See the resources listed in note #1, this chapter, particularly CUSO Education Department (1985/88).

11. A lever makes it possible to move objects many times your own weight. Most people have used a simple lever, such as a long plank with a stone under it. Likewise, in a social justice strategy, a "leverage point" is an opportunity for a person or group with less power to move someone or something with more power. A certain piece of legislation, a good contact in places of power, fortunate timing—all of these things can be leverage points.

12. See note #1, this chapter.

Chapter Ten

Step 6: Maintaining Hope

> My heart is moved by all I cannot save.
> So much has been destroyed.
> I have to cast my lot with those who,
> Age after age, perversely,
> With no extraordinary power,
> Reconstitute the world. (Rich 1978)

The Dream

People change. Sometimes the process involves two steps forward, one step back, or even two back, but people do change and heal and grow. People change individually and collectively, changing structures along the way. It does not even require a new generation, raised differently, to see change in a society.

When the United States invaded Grenada in 1983, I was working for an international development agency and had the privilege of speaking at length with those who had experienced firsthand the four years of the New Jewel Movement.[1] Some were Canadians, some Grenadians. During that cooperative, truly democratic period, they said people's everyday behaviour changed. Even at the level of fighting in bars or needing police to break up tussles at soccer games, people began to reflect the sense of common destiny and responsibility they felt. Ordinary events became peaceful. Violence against women declined dramatically in response to stiffer punishments and employment for all women in their own cooperatives.

When the coup and invasion of 1983 restored foreign domination, exploitation, and extreme divisions between classes, the whole thing reversed immediately. Violence returned as a daily occurrence. Women were on the streets again, without shelter or employment, working as prostitutes, fleeing violence in the workplace and at home. Whole societies can change, rapidly, for better or worse. As this example shows, it is not just individuals who change within a society, nor does social change take generations.

What we have learned can be unlearned. The question is, can it be unlearned in time, before the rich and powerful own the entire world and destroy it, before the depth of our "oppression training" makes us passively stand by and watch, or even assist in the destruction.

Idealism

Whenever I have spoken publicly about social justice, I get the response, "But that's idealistic." It is always said negatively, as a condemnation. People actually mean: "You are a fool because it's impossible" or "You are hopelessly naive." They are mistakenly opposing "idealism" and "realism." Idealism means a belief in the power of ideas to affect human life. Its opposite is materialism, the belief that only material reality can shape life. If you believe in the power of ideas, idealism is both realistic and practical.[2]

The other common response is: "Where do you get your hope?" The two responses are related. When I hear either, I know I am once again up against the North American concept of hope. In mainstream North American culture, hope is defined as a static thing. It has to do with outcomes, laying bets, guessing right, investing. You decide what you think will happen and invest your time, energy, and money there. Then, if you are right, you win; if you are not, you lose. If you say what you think will happen out loud to many people, everyone will admire you if you win and despise you if you lose. For example, there is some evidence that when the results of opinion polls are made public just before an election, they influence the vote. If this is true, it suggests that Canadians may care more about being on the winning side (and the resulting patronage) than about political parties, issues, or any other aspect of the "democratic" election process. This is an example of static hope.

Static hope reinforces consumerism and the "win/lose" assumption of financial investing. It leads people to conclude that if they have no proof that the world will change, they might as well spend their time being as happy and comfortable as possible, that is, accumulating as many material things as possible. These concepts of "happy" and "comfortable" are also static, as is this understanding of the purpose of material things.

Guessing the eventual outcome, that is, static "hope," is irrelevant to allies. A person becomes committed to social justice, including the processes of liberation and becoming an ally, out of a living concept of "happy" and "comfortable."

To people whose dreams have been crushed and whose roots have been severed, a life of living happiness, comfort, and peace looks like a discouraging, painful, struggle. And, while it can be a discouraging, painful, struggle, such a life also fills a person up; it is deeply satisfying. Living happiness, comfort, and peace open horizons, bring dreams and insights, expand vision, and create patterns, connections, and networks. At the worst moments, a person committed to social justice has to fall back on: "Well, if I stop struggling, I'll become part of the problem, and I couldn't stand that." At best, the process brings great joy and companionship.

In fact, for people who are connected to their own emotions and dreams, to all other life, and the earth, there is no choice. Again, I reproduce Alice Miller's quotes where she explains that for people who have full, spontaneous access to their emotions, resistance to social injustice is simply a matter of being themselves.

> Rejection, ostracism, loss of love and name calling will not fail to affect them; they will suffer as a result and will dread them, but once they have found their authentic self they will not want to lose it. And when they sense that something is being demanded of them to which their whole being says no, they cannot do it. They simply cannot. (1983:84–85)

It is for those separated from themselves that work towards social justice is an intellectual choice, a matter of duty, morals, and conscience:

> Morality and performance of duty are artificial measures that become necessary when something essential is lacking. The more successfully a person was denied access to his or her feelings in childhood, the larger the arsenal of intellectual weapons and the supply of moral prostheses has to be, because morality and a sense of duty are not sources of strength or fruitful soil for genuine affection. Blood does not flow in artificial limbs; they are for sale and can serve many masters. (85)

There is a choice for these people. They can stay "safe." No wonder they see those who stand up to injustice as naive and "idealistic."

Hope is also something we can deliberately build into the structure of social change organizations. Our efforts must include intellectual processes like critique, clear thought, analysis, strategy, choices, judgement, and making distinctions. We also must have affirmation, acceptance, tolerance, pleasure, joy, humour, release, creativity, and fun. If there is too much intellectual work, participants burn out and lose hope. Too much intellectual work can also result in making judgements and distinctions within the group, with some members putting others down. On the other hand, if there is too much openness and fun, the group can be at risk of becoming confused and co-opted, unable to stick to the harder tasks of the struggle or adjust the course when the situation changes.

An effective social justice group, whatever its purpose, can only maintain its hope if a balance of these two ways of functioning is established. Unfortunately, such a balance is difficult. Splits often occur along the line between the two. Some people find others too serious or critical and feel attacked by the kind of judgements that can be made or implied in analytical thought. The "intellectual" group thinks the "fun" group is not serious enough, just not interested in being on the "political cutting edge." It is also difficult for some to give up anger as the drive behind the impulse to work for social change. Humour, fun, warmth, vision, and love are all motivations for social change too, but our culture, particularly "the left," is much more familiar with anger.

The other common reason for burnout in social change organizations is conflict. Just like in a relationship or a family, the members of a group in conflict must have the courage to name the problem and deal with it, with a skilled outside facilitator if at all possible.

I believe human beings have a need to bond and struggle together. In our society this need has been interpreted as competition and co-opted by business, politics, and professional sports, even by war. When some men remember their experiences in war, the memories are sometimes terrible, but on the other hand, they recall those years as the "best time of my life." War offers soldiers the satisfaction of bonding in struggle; this is not part, in any real form, of most of North American society. The co-opted versions divert our attention away from the real bonds and struggles, those that will decide our future as a species on this planet.

Commitment to social justice means beginning a completely unknown journey—a journey that can unfold only one step at a time, with confusion and danger along the way, and where the end is a mystery. It is a very difficult journey for anyone to enter if their upbringing and education denied them love and security or their scars make insecurity unbearable. The childrearing and education structures of our society seem to be designed to make as many people as possible carry these limitations. On the other hand, for someone who has worked at healing the scars, finding her or his own love and security, the journey is very familiar. They have already been on a similar unknown path.

My first reason for attempting this journey is the dream. This dream is a deep, driving force in me, and I know many others share it. The dream is a vision of a world I would like to live in, a world based on cooperation, negotiation, and universal respect for the innate value of every creature on earth and the Earth herself. This is a world where no one doubts that to hurt anyone or anything is to hurt yourself and those you love most, a world where everyone works to understand what the effects of everything we do will be on future generations.

The activities leading us into this dream are already underway, by millions of people, in millions of different forms. There are small, courageous experiments happening everywhere, based in local conditions, but aware of the whole world. Our recovery of hope—full-colour, three-dimensional, hard working, clear thinking, wildly radical, living hope—is our key to liberation.

Notes

1. For more information on the story of Grenada and the New Jewel Movement, see Marcus and Taber (1983) and Payne, Sutton and Thorndike (1984).
2. I am using "idealism" the way it is used in everyday conversation, not with the more exact meanings developed over time by the Idealist school of philosophy.

Glossary

Below I explain my understanding of many of the terms I use in this book.

Ableism: A social/political/economic/ideological system that allows physically able people to marginalize and exploit people with disabilities.

Aboriginal rights: Basic justice requires that the original inhabitants of a land must be able to continue to live on it and make a living from it. This right should not be taken from them by intruders or conquerors. The original inhabitants should also be able to continue their own culture, language, and traditions.

Adultery: In a patrilineal social system, men and women are considered married permanently. If either has sexual intercourse with anyone else, they have stepped outside the accepted social bounds and have "committed adultery." The punishments were traditionally much more severe for the woman because the original purpose of patrilineal marriage was to control the fathering of children. If a married woman had intercourse with another man, she might be carrying an "illegitimate" child. In matrilineal cultures, where it is only necessary to identify a child's mother, marriage is a social and economic structure not tied to sexual exclusivity. Adultery is not a problem, and there is no such thing as an "illegitimate" child.

Adultism: A social/political/economic/ideological system that allows adults to marginalize and exploit children.

African-Canadian/African-Nova Scotian: See Black/African-Canadian/African-Nova Scotian/people of colour/immigrant people/white people

Ageism: Ageism is a social/economic/political/ideological system where some have privileges or experience discrimination because of their age. It can work against a person for being too young or too old, and sometimes a person can be too young in one situation and too old in another at the same time.

Ally: A member of an oppressor group who works to end a form of oppression which gives her or him privilege. For example, a white person who works to end racism or a man who works to end sexism.

Analysis/synthesis: The process of coming to understand a situation requires both analysis and synthesis. Analysis means taking the situation apart and looking at its pieces; synthesis is the opposite—taking the various pieces and fitting them together into one picture.

Anglophone/francophone: Anglophones speak English; francophones speak French. The struggles between these two groups, dating from the English conquest of New France in the eighteenth century, is a major feature of the Canadian political landscape. People from other countries sometimes do not understand this, and some English dictionaries from the United States do not even contain the words.

Assimilation: When a conquered people "melt" into the dominant society, becoming indistinguishable, they have been assimilated.

BCE/CE: Before the Common (or Christian) Era and the Common (or Christian) Era. A way of dividing time using the traditional year of the birth of Jesus as year 1 CE. Years in the Common Era are counted forward; that is, 1920 CE comes before 1950 CE. Years before the Common Era are counted backward; that is, 1920 BCE comes after 1950 BCE.

Bisexual: See Lesbian/gay/bisexual/heterosexual

Black/African-Canadian/African-Nova Scotian/people of colour/immigrant people/white people: The language of racism is very complicated. Sometimes racism is used to refer only to systemic oppression based on colour; sometimes other forms of oppression between peoples based on language or religious tradition are included as forms of racism. For purposes of clarity in this book, I use racism to refer only to colour-based oppression. When I mean language or religious oppression, or specifically anti-semitism, I say so.

The words for groups who suffer from racism are complex as well. Some have roots in insulting terms invented by white people; others have developed out of the pride and liberation struggles of the people they name. Sometimes a name which is used with pride in one generation becomes an insulting term in another, and a new word emerges. Sometimes one sub-group develops a term of pride and other sub-groups are not comfortable with it. For example, in Halifax "Black" is still the most common dignified word used by Black people and their supporters and has been since the 1960s. The phrases "African-Canadian" and "African-Nova Scotian" are emerging to replace it. For some, "African-Canadian" and "African-Nova Scotian" represent a new surge of energy in the fight against racism; others are not yet comfortable with it. For those who are now the elders of the community, even "Black" is uncomfortably new. Their term of pride is still "Coloured," and two organizations continue to carry the name—the Home for Coloured Children and the Nova Scotia Association for the Advancement of Coloured People.

When I am speaking to someone I know, I try to use whatever term he or she prefers. Otherwise, I tend to use "Black" or "African-Nova Scotian" as I do in this book. In other cases, I try whenever possible to use the terms claimed by communities themselves—"Roma" rather than "Gypsy," "Innu" rather than "Montagnais," and so on. When I do use a word with racist roots, it is because I do not know any better. May any person or community I insult in that way please forgive and inform me. I like the term "people of colour" and so do many friends, colleagues, and writers who live outside of Nova Scotia. Many use it to make stronger connections among all who suffer from colour-based racism. However, my experience is that many people in my own community do not like the phrase. I have used it in this work, but only when it would have taken a long list to deal with the situation otherwise. I apologize to those who do not like being called "people of colour."

In order to avoid using the phrase "people of colour" locally, I have started to say "Black, Mi'kmaq, and immigrant," meaning "those who suffer from colour-based racism here in Nova Scotia." Sometimes I use that list in this book. When I use the term "immigrant" on its own, I mean people who suffer from colour-based racism in Nova Scotia because of their Asian, Latin American, African, Southern European or Middle Eastern origins. I do not want anyone to forget that white people of European origin and the community we call "indigenous Black" or "African-Nova Scotian" are also immigrants here.

Capitalists/workers: When I use the words capitalists and workers, I am making a classic Marxist distinction between the owners of the means of production and those who sell their labour to the owners. The situation in Canada is very confusing. Many people in Canada own a little piece of capital—a rental unit, a piece of land, shares in a company—and some professional workers are much more comfortable and hold much more power than some owners of the means of production, such as farmers, woodlot owners, and fishers. The situation becomes a little clearer when you consider the fact that the means of production apparently owned by farmers, fishers, and woodlot owners are in fact largely owned by the banks. In spite of the confusing line between capitalist and worker in Canada, I think the distinction is an important one to use in understanding the underlying power structures that shape our lives.

CE: See BCE/CE

Class: As explained above, under "Capitalists/workers," class lines in Canada are very confusing. Our society is stratified and increasingly unequal. People at different class levels of our society have extremely unequal levels of access to resources, say in the political system, and even say in their own lives. However, drawing the lines is not easy. Class is not simply a matter of income but of power, and power is a function of money, culture, colour, class, gender, birth, education, and social and political position. When I use class in this book, I am referring to our different levels of access to power in Canadian society; I do not try to be precise about defining what the classes are. See also Middle class.

Competition/cooperation: Competition is part of a world-view where every person is a detached individual who gets ahead of or falls behind others according to merit, luck, ability, or ruthlessness. Competition is almost a religion in North America, something that is seen as an absolute good. Cooperation, on the other hand, is part of a world-view that sees everyone and everything as connected, where no individual can get ahead or fall behind without everyone getting ahead or falling behind.

There is a spectrum of cooperative ways of doing things. On one end, negotiation can be a way for two parties to agree on something they want, while agreeing to give up other things they want. On the other end are collective methods of organization such as consensus decision making, non-hierarchical organizations, and communities that share everything.

There is a type of friendly rivalry that does not count as competition in the way I am using the word. For example, a group of children in a berry patch decide to see who can pick the most berries in half an hour, or an educational workshop includes a game that pits small groups against each other. The difference between friendly rivalry and competition is that competition results in one person or group being counted as superior to another or obtaining more rewards than another. Friendly rivalry on the other hand results in more benefits for everyone. All of the children can eat more berries because of their picking race. All participants in the workshop learn more because of the rivalry included in the learning game.

Connection: See Separation/connection

Conquest: Conquest involves using power over another person or group of people in order to control what they have—their resources, land, skills, knowledge, labour, or reproductive ability. The power used can be economic, political, social, military, or ideological.

Cooperation: See Competition/cooperation

Deaf/Hearing: Deaf people who identify with their own highly developed culture and language call themselves "Deaf," with a capital "D." The privileged group responsible for their oppression are "Hearing." When the reference is simply to someone who cannot or can hear, they are called "deaf" or "hearing."

DNA: Deoxyribonucleic acid is an acid within the nucleus of a living cell. It contains the genetic code and carries inherited characteristics from generation to generation.

Economic: This refers to anything having to do with money or wealth. Economic power is the use of money or wealth to get what a person or people want.

Elite: The small group of people at the top of the class system are the elite, who benefit from the labour, abilities, and resources of everyone else.

Employed/unemployed: Most people in Canada are dependent on employment for their livelihood. This creates a great difference in class between those who currently have a job and those who do not. The employed are not the source of oppression of the unemployed, but the employed have many privileges that the unemployed lack.

Equality: See Hierarchy/equality

Exploitation: When a person or people control another person or people, they can make use of the controlled people's assets, such as resources, labour, and reproductive ability, for their own purposes. This is exploitation. The exploiters are those who benefit, and the exploited are those who lose.

Feminist: There are many lively debates among feminists about exactly what a feminist is. I am part of these discussions and I have my opinions about what does and does not form part of a feminist ideology. However, for the purposes of this book, details are not necessary. I use the simplest possible definition: a feminist is a woman working against sexism.

First Nations: The First Nations of North America, in a broad sense, are those peoples that were here before European settlement, for example, Mi'kmaq, Malliseet, Iriquois, Mohawk, and so on. In a more narrow sense, the term First Nations refers to people who have legal status under the Indian Act. The narrow use of the term leaves out non-status Native people and both leave out the Métis people. Just as Black people's term of self-definition has moved from Coloured to Black to African-Canadian/African-Nova Scotian, First Nations people have moved from Indian to Native or Aboriginal to First Nations, although many non-status and Métis people prefer the term Native. I use both Native and First Nations, meaning First Nations in the broader sense.

Francophone: See Anglophone/francophone

Gay: See Lesbian/gay/bisexual/heterosexual

Gender/sex: Sex refers to the physical characteristics of a person which make him or her male or female. Gender makes a person male or female through a collection of socially defined traits—appearance, attitudes, roles, preferences, work, and so on. A patriarchal society has rigid gender definitions and can be disrupted when a person of one sex displays the gender traits of the other sex. Other types of societies have more fluid definitions of gender. According to a two-spirited friend, some First Nations cultures had five or seven genders, with two-spirited people forming the middle group, half female and half male in their characteristics. See Two Spirited.

Healing: Physical healing involves getting rid of damaged tissue and contaminants from the body and building new tissue to replace what has been injured. Emotional healing involves getting rid of pain, fear, and anger through the appropriate expression of them to supportive listeners and building new, healthy patterns of living to replace the old self-protective ones. Spiritual healing includes physical and emotional healing, with the addition of throwing out all the beliefs and images forced upon a person for purposes of control and replacing them with life-loving beliefs and images coming from deep inside and deep in the roots of the individual's culture. Since an individual person cannot be fully healthy in a sick society, all of these forms of healing eventually demand that the person become involved in a collective healing process, that is, in building a healthier society.

Hearing: See Deaf/Hearing

Heterosexism/homophobia: Heterosexism refers to the structures of society that favour one kind of loving—between one man and one woman in a monogamous marriage with children—over all others. Heterosexism oppresses gay, lesbian, and bisexual people, transgendered people, two-spirited people, single people, one-parent families, unmarried couples, childless couples, and anyone else who does not fit the ideal mold. Homophobia is an individual reaction to gay, lesbian, and bisexual people—a reaction of hatred, fear, or discomfort—acted out through discrimination and violence.

Heterosexual: See Lesbian/gay/bisexual/heterosexual, also Transgendered and Two-Spirited.

Hierarchy/equality: Hierarchy is a social arrangement where some have more status and power than others. Equality is a social structure based on everyone having equal value and equal access to power. In fact, equality requires a different definition of power from that used in a hierarchy. Equality does not mean everyone is the same or that everyone has exactly the same degree of power at all times. Equal social systems are very flexible and mobile, with different people taking different forms of power at different times. However, the goal is to have it all even out over time; no one is allowed to exploit another.

Homophobia: See Heterosexism/homophobia

Ideological: This is the element of society that has to do with ideas—what people believe, value, and understand to be true and real, right and wrong, accepted limits. Ideological power is the ability to shape what people think, believe, and value.

Illegitimate children: These are children whose parents were not legally married when they were born. The concept only exists in patriarchal societies, because marriage in such systems exists to ensure control over the fathering of children. In other societies it is the mother who is more important and, consequently, all children who have a mother are legitimate; that is, all children![1]

Immigrant people: See Black/African-Canadian/African-Nova Scotian/people of colour/immigrant people/white people

Intercourse: This takes place when a man enters another person with his penis. This is an extremely important act in patriarchal societies because it defines who belongs to that man, who has been conquered by him. For women and children in Western societies, it defines who is "pure" and "undefiled" and who is not. Again, in societies that are not patriarchal, the entry of a man's penis into another person's body does not have the same power to define social relations.[2]

Internalized oppression: Oppressed people usually come to believe the negative things that are said about them and even act them out. This is called "internalized oppression." No other form of liberation can get very far unless the participants in the struggle are also freeing themselves from these negative beliefs about themselves.

Lesbian/gay/bisexual/heterosexual: As with feminism, there are lively debates, among people of all sexual orientations, about what exactly defines lesbians, gay men, bisexuals, and heterosexuals. Again, I have my own opinions, but they are not particularly important for understanding this book. Put very simply, lesbians are women who relate, emotionally and sexually, primarily to other women. Gay men relate intimately primarily to other men. Bisexual people are men or women who relate with equal depth to either men or women. Heterosexuals are men or women who relate intimately primarily to people of the opposite sex. See Heterosexism/homophobia, Transgendered, and Two-Spirited.

Liberal: Individually, every person has her or his own particular ideological system; that is, beliefs, values, world-view, and so on. Individual ideological systems can be grouped into collective ideological systems using certain key traits. One of these is the way of thought generally called "liberal."

Historically, liberal ideology comes from the time of the "liberal" revolutions—French and American—that overthrew monarchies and brought a merchant "middle" class to power. It was originally defined as an economic theory by Adam Smith in *The Wealth of Nations*, published in 1776. The key principle was no government intervention in economic matters. Wealth, according to this theory, comes from "free" enterprise, "free" competition, and "free" trade. After 1870, liberalism was modified by thinkers who believed that it was appropriate for government to regulate economic matters to a certain degree and intervene in the social realm to prevent conflict. In the 1930s, this form of modified liberalism, as defined by John Maynard Keynes, inspired the "New Deal" of the Franklin Roosevelt government in the United States. Since about 1975, however, many powerful political and economic players have worked to return liberalism to its roots. Generally called "neo-liberalism" this philosophy promotes a "free" market with no state intervention, cutting of expenditures for social services, deregulation, privatization, and elimination of the concept of "the public good." Because of the changes liberalism has gone through during its 250-year history, the term is now sometimes confusing, with different connotations in Europe and the United States.

When I use the term in this book, I am referring to an ideological system defined primarily by its belief in individuality. Equality of individuals in this way of thinking is a given, something already achieved or achievable with some reform. Liberal systems put a great deal of emphasis on individual freedom and negotiated common solutions to common problems. However, because liberals see people and groups as basically equal, the negotiations often fail to recognize the unequal resources and power of different parties. Liberal societies are shaped by those who have power, money, and historical advantages, because it is assumed that they get their way through merit. Liberals are reluctant to recognize historical and structural inequalities.

In a liberal democracy, decisions are made by majority vote. This system totally ignores the patterns of who votes and who does not; who can purchase the means of influence and who cannot; who has historical reasons to believe they will be heard in the process if they take an active part and those whose history has taught them not to bother because they will not be heard anyway; and other inequalities in the process. Liberals believe in tolerance of all differences, views and opinions, with no judgment. In fact, liberals often deny differences all together. This makes liberals wonderful, kind, accepting friends and relatives, but it also means that the more powerful forces in a liberal society are free to increase their power without being judged or limited.

Liberal ideology is the dominant one in Canada. To the right of liberal thought is the conservative minority, who believe in a God-given hierarchy that is the only "right" way to run a society. To the left is the progressive, or radical, minority who believe that equality is yet to be achieved and requires radical systemic change. Sometimes the conservative and radical minorities in Canada are more comfortable with each other than with the liberal majority, in spite of their opposed views—at least both groups have a sense of right and wrong that can be defined. Liberals are much harder, if not impossible, to pin down. The experience of social change workers in Canada is often one of "trying to nail jelly to the wall."[3]

Liberation: When an oppressed or exploited group or individual moves to change their situation, they are participating in a process of liberation. Sometimes the goal is to reverse the exploiting roles, sometimes it is to change the whole system of exploitation into one of cooperation. Both are still called liberation in common English. When I use the word I mean only the struggle to change exploitation to cooperation.

Marginalized/margins: Groups that have a history of oppression and exploitation are pushed further and further from the centres of power that control the shape and destiny of the society. These are the margins of society, and this is the process of marginalization.

Matrilineal: A social system where children trace their ancestry and take their name from their mother.

Mentally challenged: See Physically or mentally challenged

Middle class: I usually put the term "middle class" in quotation marks because I am deliberately using the term inaccurately. According to Marx, the middle class is made up of those who own wealth such as land, factories, or rental properties. In other words, the middle class is the capitalist class. However, many Canadians use the term vaguely. Most often we use it when referring to white-collar workers, people with a university degree, or people whose income is above the poverty level but below "rich." In anti-poverty work, "middle class" has come to mean those who have an education and/or a job and are, at least for the time being, out of poverty. The "middle class" are those who can be allies to those living in poverty. In this book, I am using the term in this way.

Military: This refers to armies, police, or other armed forces. Military power is the use of armed forces.

Misogyny: See Sexism/misogyny

Monogamous: Sexuality within a monogamous relationship is limited to two people. Within a patriarchal system, monogamous relationships between one man and one woman are the only acceptable kind. See Heterosexism/homophobia.

Multinational or transnational corporation: A multinational or transnational corporation (often abbreviated to simply "multinational" or "transnational") is a large company or group of companies operating in more than one country. They often have vast economic power, which they use to obtain political, military, and ideological power. In this century multinationals have achieved power beyond the control of any individual government. In fact, they control some governments and heavily influence others. They are the most powerful institutions in the world today.

Mythology: A collection of beliefs and stories about the past or about a group of people in the present. These beliefs and stories are a powerful part of ideology.

North: See South/North

Oppression/oppressor/oppressed: Oppression occurs when one group of people uses different forms of power to keep another group down in order to exploit them (or an individual keeps another down for the same purpose). The oppressor uses the power; the oppressed are exploited.

Pagan: A person who follows one of the old earth-based religions. The term comes from the Latin word for "countryside" and developed during the centuries when European cities and educated classes had become Christian, but the rural people still followed the old ways.

Patriarchy: Put most simply, patriarchy is a system where males are dominant.

Patrilineal: A social system where children trace their ancestry and take their name from their father.

People of colour: See Black/African-Canadian/African-Nova Scotian/people of colour/immigrant people/white people

People with disabilities: The large and varied group known as people with disabilities includes people who suffer from completely different forms of oppression. Those who move with the aid of wheelchairs face very different types of discrimination from those who suffer chronic pain, those whose mental abilities are different from the majority, or those who are Deaf. Often, all the different disability-based oppressions should not be thrown together, when advocating for services, for example. Any joint action among the various groups must be organized carefully, as a coalition rather than one group with completely common interests. However, for purposes of analyzing the underlying patterns of oppression, I have put all the different forms of disability-based oppression together, because I feel that they all have a common base—a society which has war-making at its heart and therefore highly values physical ability. Friends who suffer from this form of oppression have taught me that it is important to say, "people with disabilities" rather than "disabled people." The latter suggests that people with disabilities are not complete as people.

Physically or mentally challenged: This refers to a person whose oppression is based on a physical or mental difference. The able-bodied are those who are privileged by oppression of the physically challenged. I do not know a word for those who are privileged by oppression of the mentally challenged. I use the phrase physically or mentally challenged as well as the older term, people with disabilities.

Political: In Nova Scotia, when people use the term "political," they are usually referring to a connection with a political party. I use the word much more broadly, including any activity that gives a person or group more or less voice in the process of making decisions that affect the society we live in.

Popular education: Also called "Action/Reflection Learning" and

"Conscientization," this is a "school" of adult education based on a social-ist understanding of class and oppression. It is directed at people who are marginalized from the resources and benefits of society. It's aim is to help people question the world-view that they learn from the oppressor, replac-ing it with analysis and action for social change based on the experience of the oppressed.

Unlike most other forms of adult education, the action component is integral. Learning in popular education is depicted as a cycle or spiral including experience, reflection, analysis and action. The spiral is illus-trated on the first page of Chapter Nine. Developed in Africa, Latin America, and Asia, popular education came to North America primarily through voluntary international development and solidarity organizations. The main theorist associated with this school is Paulo Freire (1972) (1973) (1974). Some resources for popular education are listed in Chapter Nine, note #1.

Prejudice: See Racism/prejudice

Private ownership: Private ownership refers to an individual owning and controlling the means of production, that is, land, factories, and so on. The objects a person owns and uses in everyday life—clothes, a bicycle, a house, a car, a piano, and the like—are not included in private ownership. These are one's personal property.

Racism/prejudice: Racism is oppression based on colour. The term can be used to include oppression based on language or religion, but I have used other terms for these—language-based oppression, religious oppression, and anti-semitism. Racism is a social/political/economic system. The form practised by individuals is racial prejudice.

Reproductive capacity: The ability to produce the next generation. One of the purposes of sexism is to give men control over women's reproductive capacity.

Resources: Resources are what people need to accomplish anything. They include land, food, forests, fish, money, skills, information, knowledge, social mobility, and so on.

Roma or Romany people: A wandering people of Europe, originating in India, now spread all over the world. They have been severely oppressed by white European-descended people for centuries, and still are today. The outsiders' name for them is Gypsies.

Separation/connection: Separation is the basis for oppression, competition, conquest, and hierarchy. It is the belief that people are independent, and actions can be taken in isolation, without affecting everyone and everything. Connection is the opposite. It is the belief that everything is linked—nothing can happen to one that does not affect all. It is unthinkable to oppress or exploit another person in a system of connection.

Sex: See Gender/sex

Sexism/misogyny: Sexism is the political/economic/social/ideological system that oppresses women; misogyny is hatred, fear, and mistreatment of women by individual men.

Sexual orientation: This refers to a person's emotional, physical, and/or sexual attraction to people of their own or the opposite sex. See Gay/lesbian/bisexual/heterosexual, Heterosexism, Transgendered and Two-Spirited.

South/North: The world is divided into South and North as a result of centuries of colonialism. The Northern countries, particularly in Europe and North America, are industrialized and predominantly white; the Southern countries, particularly in Asia, Africa, Latin America, and the Pacific, live by selling raw materials and are populated predominantly by people of colour.

"South" is replacing the earlier descriptor "Third World." Third World began as a proud term, a self-naming by countries who chose to be outside of the Cold War divisions of East and West.[4] However, the term was picked up by North Americans and made into a hierarchy—First World (the capitalist North), Second World (the socialist North), and Third World (the South). As a result, many people of the South have rejected "Third World" along with "underdeveloped," "developing," and "less developed." All of these terms deny the process by which the North deliberately "un-develops" the South through oppression and exploitation.

Standardization: Societies centred around industrial production and war need to establish sameness—in trees, crops, manufactured goods, administrative systems, and people—for purposes of automation and control. This is one of the sources of all forms of oppression, particularly that of physically and mentally challenged people.

Straight: This is a common term for heterosexual people.

Street children: In both the South and the North, there are children (as well as adults) who are destitute and homeless. They survive as best they can by petty trading, drug dealing, or prostitution. These are "street children." There are millions of them in the world today, testimony to the low value placed on children in the world's dominant political/economic/ideological system. See Chapter Five, note #1.

Struggle: Struggle refers to the ongoing efforts of oppressed people to achieve liberation.

Synthesis: See Analysis/synthesis

Tokenism: A dominant group sometimes promotes a few members of an oppressed group to high positions and then uses them to claim there are no barriers preventing any member of that group from reaching a position with power and status. The people promoted are tokens, and the process is called tokenism. Tokens can also be used as a buffer between the dominant and oppressed groups. It is harder for the oppressed group to name the oppression and make demands when members of their own group are representing the dominant group.

Transgendered: Some people have a strong sense that they have been born into the wrong body. Their identity is female, but their body is male, or the other way around. Such people are referred to as "transgendered." Some choose to live publicly as the gender indicated by their body, some choose to dress and live as the gender of their identity, in spite of the sex of their body. Some pursue medical treatment, such as hormones and surgery, to change their body to fit their identity. Transgendered people suffer from the oppression of heterosexism. They can share in some issues with gay/lesbian/bisexual people, but in other cases, their issues are separate.

Two-Spirited: In the belief systems of some First Nations, there are more than two genders. Some have seven genders, some nine. Each of these genders involves a different combination of the characteristics Western society defines as "masculine" or "feminine." In the middle of this range of genders come people who are equally "male" and "female." These are the "two-spirited" people. In many Native cultures, two-spirited people were held in high esteem. In some, they were thought to have particular spiritual gifts and were trained to be spiritual leaders and healers. Many two-spirited people are what the mainstream culture would define as gay/lesbian/bisexual, but not all. These two terms do not define the same thing. A two-spirited nature encompasses much more than just sexual orientation. It is a complete gender identity.[5]

Unemployed: See Employed/unemployed

Violence: I use the word "violence" in the broadest sense, that is, any action by a person or group that causes harm or is against the interests of any other person or group. The extreme form of violence involves physical force, but there are more subtle means as well—threats, damage to self-esteem, humiliation, cruel humour, withholding resources, ignoring needs, making someone invisible, providing and controlling addictive substances.

White people: See Black/African-Canadian/African-Nova Scotian/people of colour/immigrant people/white people

Witch: Witch comes from the Anglo-Saxon word "wicce." Some authors say wicce means "to bend or shape," others say it simply means "wise." A witch is a spiritual leader in European pagan traditions. Witches can be male or female. Witches were once healers and female witches acted as midwives. Many people accused of being witches were imprisoned, tortured, and burned to death during the witch hunts of the fourteenth to eighteenth centuries. Most of those who were persecuted were women. After this time, pagan traditions went underground, and witches became a Halloween caricature of evil. Both the tradition and the witches are now re-emerging. See the case study on the Enclosure Movement in England in Chapter Two.

Notes
1. See Chapter Seven, note #2.
2. See Chapter Seven, note #2.
3. See Holt (1992) Martinez and Garcia (1996).
4. The term "Third World" was adopted by twenty-nine post-colonial states at the African–Asian Conference in Bandung, Indonesia, 18–24 April 1955. For more information on the conference, which eventually gave rise to the

non-aligned nations movement, see Singham and Hume (1986) and Mortimer (1980).

5.   This information was given by Tuma Young, a two-spirited Mi'kmaq gay man, at a workshop on two-spirited people, Atlantic Gay/Lesbian/Bisexual Conference, Halifax, Nova Scotia, 1993.

References

ABC. 1969. *The Eye of the Storm*. Centre for the Humanities, Distributor.

Abella, Irving. 1974. *On Strike: Six Key Labour Struggles in Canada, 1919–1949*. Toronto, ON: James Lewis and Samuel.

Allen, Paula Gunn. 1986. *The Sacred Hoop: Recovering the Feminine in American Indian Traditions*. Boston, MA: Beacon Press.

Allen, Richard. 1973. *The Social Passion: Religion and Social Reform in Canada, 1914–1928*. Toronto, ON: University of Toronto Press.

Allen, Robert C. 1992. *Enclosure and the Yeoman*. Oxford UK: Clarendon.

Altman, Denis. 1989. "Fear and Loathing." *New Internationalist* 201 (November).

American Friends Service Committee Curriculum Support—School District of Philadelphia. 1999. *Resistance in Paradise: Rethinking 100 years of US Involvement in the Caribbean and the Pacific*. Philadelphia, PA.

American Library Association. 1992. *Deafness: An Annotated Bibliography and Guide to Basic Materials*. Chicago, IL.

Anderson, Sarah (ed.). 2000. *Views from the South*. Chicago, IL: Food First Books and International Forum on Globalization.

Arnfield, John. Undated. "Geography 210 on the Web: Physical Geography and Environmental Issues" [http://www.geography.ohio-state.edu/classdocs/210/geog210.htm].

Arnold, Rick, and Bev Burke. 1983. *A Popular Education Handbook: An Educational Experience Taken from Central America and Adapted to the Canadian Context*. Ottawa, ON: CUSO; and Toronto, ON: Ontario Institute for Studies in Education—Adult Education Department.

Arnold, Rick, Deb Barndt, and Bev Burke. 1986. *A New Weave: Popular education in Canada and Central America*. Ottawa, ON: CUSO; and Toronto, ON: Ontario Institute for Studies in Education—Adult Education Department.

Arnold, Rick, Bev Burke, Carl James, D'Arcy Martin, and Barb Thomas. 1991. *Educating for a Change*. Toronto, ON: The Doris Marshall

Institute for Education and Action and Between the Lines Press.

Asher, Shirley Joseph. 1988. "The Effects of Childhood Sexual Abuse: A Review of the Issues and Evidence." In Lenore E. Walker (ed.), *Handbook on Sexual Abuse of Children: Assessment and Treatment Issues.* New York, NY: Springer.

Badgley, R.F. 1988. *Child Sexual Abuse in Canada: Further Analysis of the 1983 National Survey.* Ottawa, ON: Heath and Welfare Canada.

Barlow, Maude. 1990. *A Parcel of Rogues: How Free Trade is Failing Canada.* Toronto, ON: Key Porter.

———. 1998. *The Fight of my Life: Confessions of an Unrepentant Canadian.* Toronto, ON: Stoddart.

Barlow, Maude, and Bruce Campbell. 1991. *Take Back the Nation.* Toronto, ON: Key Porter.

———. 1996. *Straight Through the Heart: How the Liberals Abandoned the Just Society and What Canadians Can Do About It.* Toronto, ON: Harper Perennial.

Barlow, Maude, and Heather-jane Robertson. 1994 *Class Warfare: The Assault on Canada's Schools.* Toronto, ON: Key Porter.

Barlow, Maude, and Tony Clarke. 1997. *MAI The Multilateral Agreement on Investment and the Threat to Canadian Sovereignty.* Toronto, ON: Stoddart.

———. 1998a. *MAI: The Multilateral Agreement on Investment and the Threat to American Freedom.* New York, NY: Stoddart.

———. 1998b. *MAI Round 2: New Global and Internal Threats to Canadian Sovereignty.* Toronto, ON: Stoddart.

———. 2001. *Global Showdown: How the New Activists are Fighting Global Corporate Rule.* Toronto, ON: Stoddart.

Barlow, Maude, and James Winter. 1997. *The Big Black Book: The Essential Views of Conrad and Barbara Amiel Black.* Toronto, ON: Stoddart.

Barnet, Richard, and Ronald Muller. 1974. *Global Reach.* New York, NY: Simon and Schuster.

Barnett, Walter. 1979. *Homosexuality and the Bible.* Wallingford, PA: Pendle Hill Publications.

Barry, Kathleen. 1979. *Female Sexual Slavery.* New York, NY: Avon Books.

———. 1985. "Social Etiology of Crimes Against Women." In *Victimology: An International Journal* 10.

Bartlett, John. 1980. *Familiar Quotations: A Collection of Passages, Phrases and Proverbs Traced to Their Sources in Ancient and Modern Literature.* Boston, MA: Little Brown and Company.

Benderly, B. 1980. *Dancing Without Music.* New York, NY: Doubleday.

Bishop, Anne, and Valery Carvery. 1994. *Unlearning Racism: A Workshop Guide to Unlearning Racism*. Halifax, NS: OXFAM/Deveric.

Blackbridge, Persimmon, and Sheila Gilhooly. 1985. *Still Sane*. Vancouver, BC: Press Gang.

Blumenfeld, Warren J. (ed.). 1992. *Homophobia: How We All Pay the Price*. Boston, MA: Beacon Press.

Brickman, Julie. 1984. "Feminist, Non-sexist and Traditional Models of Therapy: Implications for Working with Incest." *Women and Therapy* 3.

———. 1992. "Female Lives, Feminist Deaths: The Relationship of the Montréal Massacre to Dissociation, Incest and Violence Against Women." *Canadian Psychology* 33,2 (April).

Brock-Utne, Birgit. 1973. *Sexual Suicide*. New York, NY: Quadrangle Press.

———. 1981. "The soldier and the mother." Paper prepared for UNESCO experts meeting, New Delhi, July 11–12.

Brooks, Imelda. 1991. "What I Remember: Residential School Memories Never Forgotten." *Micmac Maliseet Nations News* 2:5 (May).

Brown, Nancy. 1982. "Conditions Under Which Racial Learning Occurs." In NTL *Reading Book for Human Relations Training*. NTL Institute.

Bull, Linda. 1991. "Indian Residential Schooling: The Native Perspective." *Canadian Journal of Native Education* 18.

Butler, Sandra. 1978. *Conspiracy of Silence: The Trauma of Incest*. San Francisco, CA: Volcano Press.

Cahill, C, S.P. Llewelyn, and C. Pearson. 1991. "Long Term Effects of Sexual Abuse Which Occurred in Childhood: A Review." *British Journal of Clinical Psychology* 30.

Calhoun, Sue. 1983. *The Lockeport Lockout: An Untold Story in Nova Scotia's Labour History*. Halifax, NS.

Campbell, Mary. 1991. "Natives Carry Scars of Residential School." *Micmac Maliseet Nations News* 2:3 (March).

Canadian Advisory Council on the Status of Women. 1987. *Battered but not Beaten: Preventing Wife Battering in Canada*. Ottawa, ON.

Carniol, Ben. 2000. *Case Critical: Challenging Social Services in Canada*. Fourth Edition. Toronto, ON: Between the Lines.

Carty, Robert, and Virginia Smith. 1981. *Perpetuating Poverty: The Political Economy of Canadian Foreign Aid*. Toronto, ON: Between the Lines.

Castilho, Carlos. 1995. "Children to the Slaughter." [http://www.hhcr.org/wp_Jan95.htm].

Cavin, Susan. 1985. *Lesbian Origins*. San Francisco, CA: Ism Press.

Coffin Jr., William Sloan. 1983. "Homosexuality: A Sermon by Dr. William Sloan Coffin." In Committee on Gay and Lesbian Concerns, Hartford Meeting, Society of Friends, *Study Packet on Gay and Lesbian Concerns*. Hartford, MA.

Cole, Susan. 1989. *Pornography and the Sex Crisis*. Toronto, ON: Amanita.

Coles, Robert, and Jane Hallowell Coles. 1990. *Women of Crisis II*. Reading, MA: Addison-Wesley.

Committee on Sexual Offences Against Children and Youths (The Badgley Committee Report). 1984. *Sexual Offences Against Children*. Ottawa, ON: Supply and Services Canada.

Conlogue, May. 1991. "Different Views of the Montréal Massacre." *Globe and Mail*, December 4.

Counts, David R., and Dorothy A. Counts (eds.). 1991. *Coping With the Final Tragedy*. Amityville, NY: Baywood.

Courtois, Christine A. 1988. *Healing the Incest Wound: Adult Survivors in Therapy*. New York, NY: Norton.

Courtois, Christine A., and Judith E. Sprei. 1988. "Retrospective Incest Therapy for Women." In Lenore E. Walker (ed.), *Handbook on Sexual Abuse of Children*. New York, NY: Springer Publishing.

CUSO Education Department. 1985/88. *Basics and Tools: A Collection of Popular Education Resources and Activities*. Ottawa, ON.

CUSO. 1990. *Racism: A CUSO Cooperant Preparation Workshop*. Ottawa, ON.

Das Gupta, Pranab Kumar. 1989. *Life and Culture of a Matrilineal Tribe of Meghalaya*. New Delhi, India: Inter-India Publications.

Draper, Pat. 1975. "!Kung Women: Contrasts in Sexual Egalitarianism in Foraging and Sedentary Contexts." in Raya Reiter (ed.), *Toward an Anthropology of Women*. New York, NY: Monthly Review Press.

Dumanoski, Diane (citing Paul Ehrlich). 1990. "The People Problem," *Boston Globe*, February 5 [http://www.igc.apc.org/frugal/books/passion.html].

Durning, Alan. 1992. "Asking How Much Is Enough." In Brown, Lessor et al. *State of the World 1991*. New York: WW Norton. An excerpt appears in: New Roadmap Foundation, undated "All-Consuming Passion: WakingUp From the American Dream" [http://www.ecofuture.org/pk/pkar9506.html].

Dworkin, Andrea. 1981. *Pornography: Men Possessing Women*. New York, NY: Perigee Books.

Easlea, Brian. 1987. "Patriarchy, Scientists and Nuclear Warriors." In Kaufman.

Eisler, Riane. 1990. *The Chalice and the Blade*. San Francisco, CA: Harper.

Elliot, Jane. 1995. "Blue Eyed." (video, 90 minutes) California Newsreel [http://www.newsreel.org/films/blueeyed.htm, http://www.newsreel.org/guides/blueeyed.htm].

Emecheta, Buchi. 1989. "Natural Gestures." *The New Internationalist* 201 (November).

Enloe, Cynthia. 1983. *Does Khaki Become You? The Militarization of Women's Lives*. Boston, MA: South End Press.

Faderman, Lillian. 1981. *Surpassing the Love of Men: Romantic Friendship and Love Between Women from the Renaissance to the Present*. New York, NY: William Morrow.

Fidler, Richard. 1978. *RCMP: The Real Subversives*. Toronto, ON: Vanguard Publications.

Finkelhor, David. 1979. *Sexually Victimized Children*. New York, NY: Free Press.

Frank, Blye. 1987. "Hegemonic Heterosexual Masculinity." *Studies in Political Economy* 24, 15 (1987).

Freire, Paulo. 1970. *Pedagogy of the Oppressed*. New York, NY: Seabury.

———. 1972. *Cultural Action for Freedom*. Harmondsworth, UK: Penguin.

———. 1973. *Education for Critical Consciousness*. New York, NY: Seabury.

Gannon, J. 1981. *Deaf Heritage: A Narrative History of Deaf America*. Silver Spring, MD: National Association of the Deaf.

Gelday, Katherine. 1990. "The Famine Within." (video) Montréal, PQ: National Film Board of Canada, Studio D.

George, Susan. 1976. *How the Other Half Dies: The Real Reasons for World Hunger*. New York, NY: Penguin.

———. 1979. *Feeding the Few: Corporate Control of Food*. Washington, DC: Institute for Policy Studies.

———. 1984. *Ill Fares the Land: Essays on Food, Hunger, and Power*. Washington, DC: Institute for Policy Studies.

———. 1988. *A Fate Worse Than Debt*. New York, NY: Grove Press.

———. 1992. *The Debt Boomerang: How Third World Debt Harms Us All*. London, UK: Pluto.

———. 1999. *The Lugano Report: On Preserving Capitalism in the Twenty-First Century*. London, UK: Pluto.

George, Susan, and Fabrizio Sabelli. 1994. *Faith and Credit: The World Bank's Secular Empire*. Harmondsworth, UK: Penguin.

Gimbutas, Marija. 1982. *Goddesses and Gods of Old Europe*. Berkeley, CA: University of California Press.

————. 1989. *The Language of the Goddess.* San Francisco, CA: Harper and Row.

Goldstein, Martin. 1989. *Deaf Canadian: An Insight.* Calgary, AB: Martin Goldstein.

Gonner, E.C.K. 1966. *Common Land and Enclosure in England 1450–1850.* London, UK: Frank Cass.

Grahn, Judy. 1984. *Another Mother Tongue: Gay Words, Gay Worlds.* Boston, MA: Beacon Press.

Gramsci, Antonio. 1988. *Antonio Gramsci Reader: Selected writings, 1916–1935.* New York, NY: Schocker Books.

Green, Margaret. 1987. "Women in the Oppressor Role: White Racism." In Sheila Ernst and Marie Maguire (eds.), *Living with the Sphynx: Papers from the Women's Therapy Centre.* London, UK: Women's Press.

Greenberg, J. 1970. *In This Sign.* New York, NY: Holt Rinehart and Wilson.

Gruen, Arno. 1987. *The Insanity of Normality: Realism as Sickness—Toward Understanding Human Destructiveness.* New York, NY: Grove Weidenfeld.

Guillén, Ligia. 1979. *Los Niños de Nicaragua.* Costa Rica: Editorial Universitaria Centroamericana.

Halifax *Daily News.* 1993. "Pumsy the Dragon: Boosting or Brainwashing?" April 4.

Hanmer, Jalna, and Mary Maynard (eds.). 1987. *Women, Violence and Social Control.* Atlantic Highlands, NJ: Humanity Press International.

Harrison, David. 1981. *The White Tribe of Africa: South Africa in Perspective.* Berkeley, CA: University of California Press.

Health and Welfare Canada. 1991. *Foundations for the Future: A Report of the Working Group on Child and Youth Mental Health Services.* Ottawa, ON: Health Services and Promotion Branch.

Helms, Janet E. (ed.). 1990. *Black and White Racial Identity: Theory, Research, and Practice.* Westport, CN: Praeger.

Henry, Frances. 1973. *Forgotten Canadians: The Blacks of Nova Scotia.* Toronto, ON: Longman.

Hill, Christopher. 1972. *The World Turned Upside Down: Radical Ideas During the English Revolution.* New York, NY: Viking.

Hoagland, Sarah L. 1988. *Lesbian Ethics.* Palo Alto, CA: Institute of Lesbian Studies.

Holt, Chris. 1992. "Liberalism: Frequently Asked Questions." University of Newcastle upon Tyne, [http://www.cs.ncl.ac.uk/people/chris.holt/home.informal/lounge/politics/liberalism.html].

hooks, bell. 1990. *Yearning: Race, Gender and Cultural Politics*. Toronto, ON: Between the Lines.

Ing, Roslyn. 1991. "The Effects of Residential Schooling on Native Child-rearing Practices." *Canadian Journal of Native Education* 18.

International Panel on Climate Change. 2001. *Third Assessment Report*. Four volumes. Cambridge, UK: Cambridge University.

Jackins, Harvey. 1973. *The Human Situation*. Seattle, WA: Rational Island Publishers.

Jacobs, L,A. 1980. *A Deaf Adult Speaks Out*. Washington, DC: Gallaudet College Press.

James, Carl. 1989. *Seeing Ourselves: Exploring Race, Ethnicity and Culture*. Toronto, ON: Sheridan College.

Jensen, Robert. 1998. "White People Need to Acknowledge Benefits of Unearned Privilege." *Baltimore Sun*. [http://www.dickshovel.com/priv.htm]. Go to www.dickshovel.com, enter it, go through introductory pages, open "First Nations Site Search Tool," type in "Jensen, Robert."

———. 1999. "More Thoughts on Why the System of White Privilege is Wrong." *Baltimore Sun* July 4 [http://www.dickshovel.com/priv2.htm]. Go to this site, enter it, go through introductory pages, open "First Nations Site Search Tool," type in "Jensen, Robert."

Johnson, Beverly D. 1991. *Black Perspectives on Foster Care: A Project Exploring the Experience of Foster Care Placement on Black Children Placed in White Foster Homes*. MSW Thesis, Maritime School of Social Work, Dalhousie University, Halifax, NS.

Johnson, Carl E.K. 1988. "Retrospective Incest for Men." In Lenore E. Walker (ed.), *Handbook on Sexual Abuse of Children: Assessment and Treatment Issues*. New York, NY: Springer.

Kannapell, Barbara. 1980. "Personal Awareness and Advocacy in the Deaf Community." In C. Baker and R. Battison (eds.), *Sign Language and the Deaf Community: Essays in Honor of William C. Stokoe*. Silver Spring, MD: National Association of the Deaf.

Katz, Judith. 1978. *White Awareness: Handbook for Anti-racism Training*. Norman, OK: University of Oklahoma Press.

Kaufman, Michael (ed.). 1987. *Beyond Patriarchy: Essays By Men on Pleasure, Power, and Change*. New York, NY: Oxford University Press.

Kaye, Marcia. 1991. "The Nightmare of Childhood Sexual Abuse can Last a Lifetime but Increasingly, Adult Survivors are Waking to Renewed Hopes and Dreams." *Canadian Living Magazine* 16, 3 (March).

Kinzer, Stephen. 1991. *Blood of Brothers: Life and War in Nicaragua*. New

York, NY: Doubleday.

Kirkham, Kate. 1988/89. "Teaching About Diversity: Navigating the Emotional Undercurrents." *The Organizational Behavior Teaching Review* 13, 4.

Kleinberg, Seymour. 1987. "The New Masculinity of Gay Men." In Kaufman.

Kneen, Brewster, 1993. *From Land to Mouth, Second Helping: Understanding the Food System*. Toronto, ON: NC Press.

Knockwood, Isabelle, with Gillian Thomas. 1992. *Out of the Depths: The Experiences of Mi'kmaw Children at the Indian Residential School at Shubenacadie, Nova Scotia*. Lockeport, NS: Roseway Publishing.

Kohn, Alfie. 1986. *No Contest: The Case Against Competition*. Boston, MA: Houghton Mifflin.

Kristeva, Julia. 1977. "Chinese Women: The Mother at the Centre." *Liberation* 20, 3 (March/April).

Kuyek, Joan Newman. 1990. *Fighting for Hope: Organizing to Realize our Dreams*. Montréal, PQ: Black Rose.

Ladner, Joyce A. 1977. *Mixed Families: Adopting Across Racial Boundaries*. New York, NY: Anchor Press/Doubleday.

Laidlaw, Toni Ann, Cheryl Malmo and Associates. 1990. *Healing Voices: Feminist Approaches to Therapy with Women*. San Francisco, CA: Jossey Bass.

Lalonde, Michelle. 1991. "I am not a Feminist." *Montréal Gazette*, 30 November.

Lambley, Peter. 1980. *The Psychology of Apartheid*. Athens, GA: University of Georgia Press.

Leacock, Eleanor. 1977. "The Changing Family and Levi Strauss, or Whatever Happened to the Fathers?" *Social Research* 44, 2 (Summer).

Lee, Enid. 1985. *Letters to Marcia: Anti-racist Education in School*. Toronto, ON: Cross Cultural Communication Centre.

Leemon, Thomas. 1972. *The Rites of Passage in a Student Culture*. New York, NY, and London, UK: Teachers College Press.

Leopold, Evelyn. 2000. "Canada Best Place to Live—UN Report." *Reuters* June 30.

Lerner, Harriet Goldhor. 1985. *The Dance of Anger: A Woman's Guide to Changing the Patterns of Intimate Relationships*. New York, NY: Harper and Row.

Lill, Wendy. 1987. "The Occupation of Heather Rose." In Diane Bessai and Don Kerr (eds.) *NeWest Plays by Women*. Edmonton, AB: NeWest Press.

————. 1991. *Sisters*. Vancouver, BC: Talonbooks.

Lorde, Audre. 1980. *Cancer Journals*. Argyle, NY: Spinsters Ink.

Lyttelton, Ned. 1983–84. "Men's Liberation: Men Against Sexism and Major Dividing Lines." *Resources for Feminist Research* 12, 4 (December/January).

MacKinnon, Catherine. 1987. *Feminism Unmodified: Discourses on Life and Law*. Cambridge, MA: Harvard University Press.

Malinowski, Bronislaw. 1927. *Sex and Repression in Savage Society*. Chicago, IL: University of Chicago Press.

Mann, Edward, John Allen Lee, and Norman Penner. 1979. *RCMP vs. the People: Inside Canada's Security Service*. Toronto, ON: General Publishing.

Mander, Jerry. 1991. *In the Absence of the Sacred: The Failure of Technology and the Survival of the Indian Nations*. San Francisco, CA: Sierra Club.

————. 1996. *The Case Against the Global Economy: And a Turn Toward the Local*. San Francisco, CA: Sierra Club.

Marcus, Bruce, and Michael Taber (eds.). 1983. *Maurice Bishop Speaks: The Grenada Revolution, 1979–83*. New York, NY: Pathfinder Press.

Martin, A. Damien. 1984. "The Perennial Canaanites: The Sin of Homosexuality." *Et Cetera* 41, 4.

Martinez, Elizabeth, and Arnoldo Garcia. 1996. "What is New-Liberalism? A Brief Definition for Activists." [http://www.igc.apc.org/envjustice/neolib.html].

McCaskell, Tim. 1988. "Racism as a White Problem." In *Facilitator's Handbook for Students' Multicultural/Multiracial Camp*. Toronto, ON: Toronto Board of Education.

McDougall, Sheila. 1991. "Thank God for the Shubie School." *Micmac Maliseet Nations News* 2:8 (August).

McGillivray, Don. 1990. "Men Must Face Massacre Reality." *Vancouver Sun* 19 November.

McIntosh, Peggy. 1990. "White Privilege: Unpacking the Invisible Knapsack" *Independent School* 49,2 (Winter), available on many websites, including for example [http://www.spokenhumanrights.org/CCVV/packet/article.htm]

McQuaig, Linda. 1987. *Behind Closed Doors: How the Rich Won Control of Canada's Tax System and Ended Up Richer*. Markham, ON: Viking.

————. 1991. *The Quick and the Dead: Brian Mulroney, Big Business, and the Seduction of Canada*. Toronto, ON: Penguin.

————. 1993. *The Wealthy Banker's Wife: The Assault on Equality in Canada*. Toronto, ON: Penguin.

————. 1995. *Shooting the Hippo: Death by Deficit and Other Canadian Myths*. Toronto, ON: Penguin.

————. 1998. *The Cult of Impotence: Selling the Myth of Powerlessness in the Global Economy*. Toronto, ON: Penguin.

Mellor, John. 1983. *The Company Store: James Bryson McLachlan and the Cape Breton Coal Miners, 1900–1925*. Toronto, ON: Doubleday.

Merchant, Carolyn. 1980. *The Death of Nature: Women, Ecology, and the Scientific Revolution*. San Francisco, CA: Harper and Row.

Michener, James. 1980. *The Covenant*. New York, NY: Random House.

Midnight Sun. 1988. "Sex/Gender Systems in Native North America." In Will Roscoe (ed.), *Living the Spirit: A Gay American Indian Anthology*. New York, NY: St. Martin's Press.

Mies, Maria. 1986. *Patriarchy and Accumulation on a World Scale*. London, UK: Zed Books.

————. 1993. "New Reproductive Technologies: Sexist and Racist Implications." In Mies and Shiva.

Mies, Maria, and Vandana Shiva. 1993. *Ecofeminism*. Halifax, NS: Fernwood Publishing.

Miller, Alice. 1981. *Prisoners of Childhood: The Drama of the Gifted Child and the Search for the True Self*. New York, NY: Basic Books.

————. 1983. *For Your Own Good: Hidden Cruelty in Child-rearing and the Roots of Violence*. New York, NY: Farrar, Straus and Giroux.

————. 1986. *Thou Shalt Not Be Aware: Society's Betrayal of the Child*. New York, NY: New American Library.

Milloy, John S. 1999. *A National Crime: The Canadian Government and the Residential School System 1879 to 1986*. Winnipeg, MB: University of Manitoba.

Mingay, G.E.. 1990. *A Social History of the English Countryside*. London, UK: Routledge.

————. 1997. *Parliamentary Enclosure in England: An Introduction to its Causes, Incidence, and Impact, 1750–1850*. New York, NY: Longman.

Monkman, Penny, Garth Tyler-Neher, and Joyce Tyler-Neher. 1983. "The Poverty Game." The Poverty Game. 2-956 Cornwall Crescent, Dawson Creek, British Columbia V1G 1N9.

Morgan, Dan. 1979. *Merchants of Grain*. New York, NY: Penguin.

Mortimer, Robert A. 1980. *The Third World Coalition in International Politics*. New York, NY: Praeger.

Muszynski, Alicja. 1991. "What is Patriarchy?" In Jesse Vorst et al. (eds.), *Race, Class, Gender: Bonds and Barriers, 2nd ed. (rev.)*. Winnipeg, MB: Society for Socialist Studies.

National Film Board of Canada/Alter-Cine. 1996. (video) *Hand of God, Hand of the Devil*. Part 1 of the Rwanda Series, Yvan Patry, Director [http://www.nfb.ca/alias/34981.html].

New Internationalist. 1989. "Pride and Prejudice: Homosexuality." 201 (November).

New Roadmap Foundation. 1993. *All Consuming Passion: Waking Up From the American Dream*. Seattle, WA: New Roadmap Foundation [http://www.igc.apc.org/frugal/books/passion.html].

Obear, Kathy. 1990. *Opening Doors to Understanding and Acceptance: A Facilitator's Guide to Presenting Workshops on Lesbian and Gay Issues*. Cambridge, MA: Campaign to End Homophobia.

Obedkoff, Vicki. 1989. *Exploring Racism: Workshop Materials for Congregational Groups*. Toronto, ON: The United Church of Canada.

Oja, G. 1987. *Changes in the Distribution of Wealth in Canada, 1970–1984*. Ottawa, ON: Statistics Canada, Cat. 13-588 (June).

Orbach, Susie. 1978. *Fat is a Feminist Issue: A Self-Help Guide for Compulsive Eaters*. New York, NY: Berkeley Books.

Pachai, Bridglal. 1987. *Beneath the Clouds of the Promised Land: The Survival of Nova Scotia's Blacks. Vol. 1, 1600–1800*. Halifax, NS: Black Educators Association.

Padden, Carol. 1980. "The Deaf Community and the Culture of Deaf People." In C. Baker and R. Battison (eds.), *Sign Language and the Deaf Community: Essays in Honor of William C. Stokoe*. Silver Spring, MD: National Association of the Deaf.

———. 1988. *Deaf in America: Voices From a Culture*. Cambridge, MA: Harvard University Press.

Paton, Alan. 1982. *Ah, But Your Land is Beautiful*. New York, NY: Scribner.

Payne, Anthony, Paul Sutton and Tony Thorndike. 1984. *Grenada: Revolution and Invasion*. London, UK: Croom Helm.

Pearce, Jenny. 1982. *Under the Eagle: U.S. Intervention in Central America and the Caribbean*. Boston, MA: South End Press.

Personal Counsellors Inc. 1962. *Fundamentals of Co-counselling Manual: Elementary Counsellors Manual*. Seattle, WA: Rational Island Publishers.

Peiterse, Jan Nederveen. 2000. *Global Futures: Shaping Globalization*. London, UK: Zed Press.

Peters, William. 1987. *A Class Divided, Then and Now, Expanded Edition*. New Haven, CN, and London, UK: Yale University.

Petras, James, and Morley Morris. 1975. *The United States and Chile: Imperialism and the Overthrow of the Allende Government*. New York,

NY: Monthly Review Press.

Pharr, Suzanne. 1988. *Heterosexism: A Weapon of Sexism*. Oakland, CA: Chardon Press.

Plant, Roger.1978. *Guatemala: An Unnatural Disaster*. London, UK: Latin American Bureau.

Pogrebin, Letty Cottin. 1991. "Ain't We Both Women? Blacks, Jews and Gender." In *Deborah, Golda and Me: Being Female and Jewish in America*. New York, NY: Crown Publishers.

Raghavan, Iyer. 1973. *The Moral and Political Thought of Mahatma Gandhi*. New York, NY: Oxford Press.

Reynolds, Malvina. 1975. "World in their Pocket." New York: Schroeder Music.

Rich, Adrienne. 1978. *The Dream of a Common Language: Poems 1974–77*. New York, NY: Norton.

———. 1986. *Your Native Land, Your Life: Poems*. New York, NY: Norton.

Richardson, Boyce (ed.). 1989. *Drumbeat: Anger and Renewal in Indian Country*. Toronto, ON: Summerhill Press.

———. 1997. "Corporations: How Do We Curb Their Obscene Power?" "MAI? No Thanks! On-Line Library" [http://www.geocities/com/athens/3565/mai/cancorp1.html].

Rose, Suzanna. 1991. "The Contribution of Alice Miller to Feminist Therapy and Theory." *Women and Therapy* 11, 2.

Royal Commission on Aboriginal Peoples. 1996. *Report of the Royal Commission on Aboriginal Peoples, Chapter 10*. Ottawa, ON: Minister of Supply and Services Canada. All 3200 pages of the report are available on-line at the Institute of Indigenous Government website [http://www.indigenous.bc.ca].

Sacks, Oliver. 1990. *Seeing Voices: A Journey into the World of the Deaf*. London, UK: Pan Books.

Salutin, Rick. 1980. *Kent Rowley, The Organizer: A Canadian Union Life*. Toronto, ON: Lorimer.

Sanders, Richard. 1996. "Community Education in Peace Activism." *Peace and Environment News* December [http://www.perc.ca/PEN/1996-12-01/sanders.htm].

Sawatsky, John. 1980. *Men in the Shadows: The RCMP Security Service*. Toronto, ON: Doubleday.

Scheff, Thomas J. 1979. *Catharsis in Healing, Ritual, and Drama*. Berkeley, CA: University of California.

Schlegal, Alice. 1984. "Hopi Gender Ideology of Female Superiority." *Quarterly Journal of Ideolog* 8, 4 (October).

Schlenker, Jon A. 1975. "An Historical Analysis of the Family Life of the Choctaw Indians." *Southern Quarterly* 13, 4 (July).

Schoepf, Brook-Grundfest. 1987. "Social Structure, Women's Status and Sex Differential Nutrition in the Zairian Copperbelt." *Urban Anthropology* 16, 1 (Spring).

Sherr-Klein, Bonnie, and Linda-Lee Tracy. 1981. "Not a Love Story" (video). Montréal: National Film Board of Canada, Studio D.

Shiva, Vandana. 1993. *Monocultures of the Mind*. London, UK: Zed Press.

———. 1997. *Biopiracy: The Plunder of Nature and Knowledge*. Cambridge, MA: South End Press.

———. 1999. *Stolen Harvest: The Hijacking of the Global Food Supply*. Cambridge, MA: South End Press.

———. 2001. *Water Wars: Pollution, Profits, and Privatization*. Cambridge, MA: South End Press.

Simon, Rita J., and Howard Alstein. 1992. *Adoption, Race, and Identity from Infancy Through Adolescence*. New York, NY: Praeger.

Singham, A.W., and Shirley Hume. 1986. *Non-alignment in an Age of Alignments*. London, UK: Zed Books.

Slater, Gilbert. 1907 (1968 reprint). *The English Peasantry and the Enclosure of Common Fields*. New York, NY: Augustus M. Kelley.

Smith, William. 1978. *The Meaning of Conscientization: The Goal of Paulo Freire's Pedagogy*. Boston, MA: University of Massachusetts.

Snodgrass, Jon (ed.). 1977. *A Book of Readings for Men Against Sexism*. Albion, CA: Times Change Press.

Some Angry Women. 1992. "Why Did Jane Hurshman Have to Die?" *New Maritimes* 10, 6 (July/August).

Sparks, Allister. 1990. *The Mind of South Africa*. New York, NY: Knopf.

Starhawk. 1982. *Dreaming the Dark: Magic, Sex and Politics*. Boston, MA: Beacon Press.

———. 1987. *Truth or Dare: Encounters With Power, Authority, and Mystery*. San Francisco, CA: Harper and Row.

———. 1993. *The Fifth Sacred Thing*. New York, NY: Bantam (fiction).

Statistics Canada. 2001. *The Assets and Debts of Canadians: An Overview of the Results of the Survey on Financial Security*. Cat # 13-595-XIE, based on 1999 data, released March 15, 2001. There is a brief summary on the Statistics Canada website at [http://www.statcan.ca/Daily/English/010315/d010315a.htm] and the report can be downloaded free, also from the Statistics Canada website [http://www.statcan.ca.80/english/IPS/Data/13-595-XIE.htm].

Statistics Canada and Lars Osberg. 1981. *Economic Inequality in Canada*.

Toronto, ON: Butterworth.

Steinem, Gloria. 1992. *The Revolution From Within: A Book About Self Esteem*. Boston, MA: Little, Brown and Co.

Swanson, Jean. 2001a. *Poor-bashing: The Politics of Exclusion*. Toronto, ON: Between the Lines.

———. 2001b. "Gap Between Rich and Poor Expands." *The Long Haul* VIII,1 (April).

Swenarchuk, Michelle. 1999. *Liberalized Investment and Investor-State Suits: Threats to Government Powers*. Toronto, ON: Canadian Environmental Law Association.

Swift, Richard, and Robert Clarke (eds.). 1982. *Ties That Bind: Canada and the Third World*. Toronto, ON: Between the Lines.

Thomas, Barb. 1984. "Principles of Anti-racist Education." *Currents: Readings in Race Relations* 2, 3 (Fall).

Thomas, Barb, and Charles Novogrodsky. 1983a. *Combatting Racism in the Workplace: A Course for Workers*. Toronto, ON: Cross Cultural Communication Centre.

———. 1983b. *Combatting Racism in the Workplace: Readings Kit*. Toronto, ON: Cross Cultural Communication Centre.

Thompson, Allan. 1997. "Canada Still Best Place to Live." *Toronto Star*, June 12 [http://canada-acsus.plattsburgh.edu/Unreport.htm].

Thompson, Cooper. 1990. *A Guide to Leading Introductory Workshops on Homophobia*. Cambridge. MA: Campaign to End Homophobia.

Thwaites, R.C. (ed.). 1906. *The Jesuit Relations and Allied Documents, 71 volumes*. Cleveland, OH: Burrows Brothers.

Tolson, Andrew. 1977. *The Limits of Masculinity*. London, UK: Tavistock.

Troiden, Richard. 1988. *Gay and Lesbian Identity: A Sociological Analysis*. Dix Hills, NY: General Hall.

United Nations Development Program. 1998. *Human Development Report 1998*. New York, NY: Oxford University Press.

Velasquez, Mauricio. 1998. "Success vs. Failed Diversity Programs." Herndon, VA: The Diversity Training Group [http://diversitydtg.com/articles/topten.html].

Villamarin, Juan A. 1975. "Kinship and Inheritance Among the Sabana de Bogota Chibcha at the Time of the Spanish Conquest." *Ethnology* 14, 2.

Walker, James St. G. 1980. *A History of Blacks in Canada*. Ottawa, ON: Supply and Services Canada.

Ware, Eugene F.. 1960. *The Indian War of 1864*. New York, NY: St. Martin's Press.

Winks, Robin. 1971. *The Blacks in Canada: A History*. New Haven, CT, and London, UK: Yale University Press.

Winter, James, and Amir Hassanpour. 1994. "Building Babel." *Canadian Forum* LXXll: 826 (January/February).

World Health Organization. 1993. "A One-Way Street? Report on Phase 1 of the Street Children's Program." [http://www.hhcr.org/Who1.htm].

Wright, Ronald. 1992. *Stolen Continents: The "New World" Through Indian Eyes*. Harmondsworth, UK: Penguin.

Yalnizyan, Armine. 1998. *The Growing Gap: A Report on Growing Inequality Between Rich and Poor in Canada*. Toronto, ON: Centre for Social Justice.

Yarrow, Matthew. 1999. *Still Pulling Strings: the US Military in Latin America after the Cold War*. Philadelphia, PA: American Friends Service Committee.

Yelling, J.A. 1977. *Common Field and Enclosure in England 1450–1850*. London, UK: Macmillan.

Index

50. *Also see* Summit of the Americas, Québec City, April 2001

Canada—child abuse statistics, 62–63

Canada—class structure, 154, 155, 160

Canada—dominant ideology, 160

Canada—growing gap between rich and poor, 51

Canada—impact of globalization, 47

Canada—international reputation, 55

Canada—media ownership, 53

Canada—political repression, 54–55

Canada—role in defeating Multilateral Agreement on Investment, 50

Canada—trade disputes under the North American Free Trade Agreement, 50

child abuse, 29, 33, 59, 61–73, 88, 96, 97, 98

child sexual abuse. *See* child abuse

childbirth, 100

children, 28, 29, 34, 41, 42, 52, 80, 82, 85, 87, 90, 95, 101, 103, 110, 148, 149, 151, 157, 160, 162. *Also see* adultism, child abuse, children—illegitimate, children as property, street children

children as property, 28, 29, 32, 42, 89, 158. *Also see* women as property

children—illegitimate, 151, 158

class, 11, 14, 19, 21, 27, 30, 31, 32, 35, 36, 37, 38, 42, 47, 48, 51, 52, 55, 71, 72, 73, 81, 84, 87, 88, 110, 115, 125, 146, 153, 154, 155, 159, 160, 163. *Also see* Canada—class structure, economic aspects of class, globalization, growing gap between rich and poor, ideological aspects of class, political aspects of class

collective action, 96, 104, 125. *Also see* social justice activists

competition, 11, 18–19, 20, 21, 25, 26, 29, 30, 42, 51, 53, 66, 71, 78, 86, 90, 102, 104, 149, 154, 159, 164

conflict, 149

conflict in social justice "social justice activists" groups, 11

conflict in social justice groups, 42–44, 60–73, 99, 149

connection, 18, 25, 43, 97, 101, 102, 111, 118, 155, 164

conquest, 26, 28, 30, 34, 42, 43, 61, 91, 97, 152, 155, 164

consciousness, 22, 70, 99, 102, 103, 104, 112, 120

consensus decision-making, 18, 43, 60, 61, 71, 98, 103, 154

conspiracy theory, 48

cooperation, 18, 19, 20, 25, 30, 42, 44, 71, 134, 150, 154, 155, 160

cultural memories, 96

culture, 14, 19, 27, 28, 29, 30, 31, 32, 38, 42, 43, 44, 47, 52, 53, 55, 61, 62, 64, 66, 67, 71, 72, 73, 76, 80, 82, 84, 90, 92, 101, 104, 112, 113, 125, 147, 149, 151, 154, 155, 156, 157, 166

D

Deaf people, 79, 90, 92, 155, 162. *Also see* ableism

defensiveness, 109, 112, 115, 116, 123, 128, 134, 135

differences among different forms of oppression, 79–84

Diggers, 35, 36, 37, 41

disability based oppression. See ableism

distinctions within the major oppressions, 90–92

diversity education, 11, 126, 127

divide and conquer, 18, 20, 51, 98

hierarchy, 19, 25, 26, 27, 28, 29, 32, 34, 42, 51, 53, 65, 67, 71, 72, 73, 78, 82, 84, 101, 103, 154, 156, 157, 160, 164

homophobia. See heterosexism

hope, 11, 12, 19, 20, 22, 107, 143, 146–50

human rights, 80, 81

humour, 85, 98, 149, 166

I

idealism, 147–48

ideological aspects of class, 82, 84

ideological power, 51, 53, 89, 97, 155, 158, 161

ideological separation of parents and children, 88

ideological structures/systems, 110, 159

ideological, definition, 158

ideological/cultural social justice tactics, 82, 84

ideology, 27, 36, 38, 71, 161

Indian residential schools, 26, 29, 33, 34, 71, 72, 77, 89

individuals reproducing oppression, 12, 65, 60–73, 96, 98, 111–12, 149

Innu (Montagnais-Naskapi) people, 32–34, 72, 153

Inquisition, 80, 96

internalized oppression, 29, 47, 53, 73, 82, 89, 116, 125, 158

internalized oppressor attitudes, 119

International Monetary Fund, 48, 50

J

Jewish people, 20, 67, 85, 88, 96, 111, 120, 123. *Also see* anti-semitism

K

Kurdish people, 96

L

labour exploitation, 19, 27, 28, 47, 154, 155, 156

labour unions, 20, 54, 134

language based oppression, 14, 65, 78, 83, 123, 130, 131, 151, 152, 163

lesbian oppression. See heterosexism

liberal, 11, 19, 86, 125, 126, 127, 159

liberation, 11, 12, 20, 22, 78, 79, 90, 96, 100, 102, 104, 111, 112, 114, 116, 117, 121, 123, 125, 126, 147, 150, 153, 158, 160, 165

M

majority rule, 43, 53, 159

matrilineal systems. *See* patrilineal/matrilineal systems

media, 26, 49, 51, 63, 85, 88, 89

media ownership, 53

memory suppression and recovery, 62, 66, 68, 95, 97

Mi'kmaw (Mi'kmaq) people, 81, 90, 118, 153

military power, 25, 51, 52, 155, 161

Montréal Massacre, 121

Multilateral Agreement on Investment, 51

multinational corporations. See transnational corporations

myth of objective information, 52

myth of scarcity, 52

N

Native people, 16, 26, 32–34, 54, 64, 69, 72, 73, 76, 80, 87, 88, 89, 90, 96, 123, 156, 166

nature, 25, 26, 27, 31, 38, 40, 47, 48, 80, 101, 102

neo-liberalism. See liberal

North American Free Trade Agreement, 50